Hot Pursuit:

Chase Your Dreams with Passion and Live an Exceptional Life

MELISSA V. WEST

ISBN-13:978-1530003204

ISBN-10:1530003202

Endorsements

It's not often you find a person who doesn't take no for an answer when pursuing their dreams. Many will talk about not taking "No" for an answer but very few will go through the growth pains it takes to do it. I have always said who you learn from matters. Find someone who has done what they teach and you are sure to learn from a master. When it comes to pursuing and achieving your dreams, Melissa is a master. - **Paul Martinelli, President of the John Maxwell Team**

We all live with tension over the difference between what we want and we are. Melissa has lived that tension, made incredible changes to her personal journey, and exited with a mission to give others the gift of living their dreams. She now turns her extensive experience into a roadmap to get you to your desired destination. Her expertise in coaching and mentoring others shines as she outlines practical and attainable steps to take you from here to there. - **Alan Hoffler, Public speaking coach and trainer, MillsWyck Communications**

Melissa West is a master storyteller, and *Hot Pursuit* is her best so far, because it is her story! She describes her journey in inspiring ways, without sugarcoating away the challenges, fears and doubts. If you want a book that makes you laugh (a lot), cry (a little) and come away with a renewed commitment to make the rest of your life the best of your life, *Hot Pursuit* is it! I highly recommend this book, and promise that you will benefit greatly from Melissa's lessons. - **Ed DeCosta, Executive Coach**

In a world where most dreams suffer a stillbirth, Melissa West made hers a reality when all the conditions, circumstances and people around her said it couldn't be done. We all have chapters we would rather keep unpublished, and that's what makes *Hot Pursuit* such an important read for you - it's real. It's not some dressed up theory full of concepts and ideologies. This is life, warts and all. And I can assure you, you'll be a much better person for having read it **– Christian Simpson, UK's Leading Coach & Mentor to Entrepreneurs**

Melissa shares her courageous story because she is passionate about giving you the tools you need to live your dreams. Hot Pursuit will not only challenge you to dream bigger, but it will inspire you to chase your destiny. **- Audrey Moralez, Writer and Content Coach, Audrey Moralez.com**

This book is dedicated to Paul Martinelli – my friend, mentor, and business partner.

Paul, you have taught me more about life and business than anyone else on this planet. You have been my encourager and supporter and given me more opportunities than I feel I deserve. Thank you for always believing in me.

Table of Contents

Acknowledgments

A big hearty THANK YOU to all who have been on this crazy *Hot Pursuit* journey with me! I am blessed to have so many amazing people in my life rooting me on.

Thank you to my husband, best friend, and greatest fan, Christopher West. He not only supported me every step of the way (as he always does), but stepped into his greatness as a father. He and our daughter, Olivia, had some great times at the park and story time at the library while mommy was home writing.

Thank you to my writer, Audrey Moralez who helped me take my story and transform it into a masterpiece. She wasn't just a writer to me, but also a thinking partner and friend. She helped me think through some tough decisions along the way, kept me on track, and kept me sane.

Thank you to my mentors who have poured so much wisdom into me over the years. I would not be where I am today without them. Thank you Paul Martinelli, John C. Maxwell, Scott M. Fay, Ed DeCosta, Christian Simpson, and Roddy Galbraith.

I would also like to acknowledge those who contributed to the making of this book. You stepped up right away to help me brainstorm ideas, proofread, edit, and encourage me. Thank you to Carol Gates, Brian Simpson, Teresa Molter, and Cory Reed.

Author's Note

In my late twenties, I had a life of abundant *goodness*. I had a good job, good friends, and a good relationship with my family and co-workers. I worked for a good company, enjoyed good benefits, and was paid a good salary. I worked hard and my life looked exactly how I expected it to look.

Yes, it was a *good life*, but *my good life* had come at the expense of the *great life* I was created to live. Somewhere along the way, I'd stopped asking what I *really wanted out of life*. Maybe I'd never asked myself what I wanted in the first place. Either way, something was missing.

Have you ever felt that way? Do you crave more out of life? More joy? More passion? More fulfillment? Is there a part of you that knows that there's more to life than the life you're living right now? Do you hold a dream in your heart but feel far away from achieving it? Are you pursuing your dream but feeling discouraged by some of the roadblocks and obstacles you've encountered along the way?

If so, then this book was written with you in mind – because no matter how *good* your life is, I believe you're meant for more. My journey began with the nagging sense that I wasn't living the best life I could live. Have you experienced the same "nagging" feeling? I hope so. My greatest wish for you is that you *never stop* wanting more from yourself and your life.

Thankfully, I paid attention to my intuition. As a result, my life is far better than anything I could have imagined at the time. Today, I have the privilege of speaking, coaching, and training thousands around the world. I lead transformation initiatives in countries like Guatemala and Paraguay. I'm a faculty member of The John Maxwell Team, the largest leadership development organization in the world. I've partnered with incredible people like Paul Martinelli and John C. Maxwell. And the best part of all? My family life is amazing. I'm happily married with a beautiful daughter and a new baby on the way. Sometimes I have to pinch myself and ask, *Is this really my life?!?*

None of this would have been possible if I hadn't made the choice to go after my dreams. That's why I'm so passionate about sharing my story with you. I may not know the dreams that burn inside of you, *but I know you are destined to live an exceptional life.* If you don't believe it, then borrow some of my belief. I believe it enough for both of us!

My dreams came true because I dared to hope I could make them a reality. *Now it's your turn.* Believe me, if I can do it, so can you. I'm just a small town girl from Wisconsin. I am not smarter or better resourced than you. There was a time when I had no idea what my dream was, let alone how to achieve it. But I kept asking questions. And I continued to search until I found answers.

Through my own experience, and through coaching thousands of others on their journeys, this is what I've learned:

To find true, lasting happiness you must pursue the dream in your heart.

That's why I've named this book *Hot Pursuit*. Because it isn't enough to hope and wish you'll stumble on more meaning and joy. It isn't enough to say you want more out of life, but not be willing to do what it takes to attain it. If you want more, then you have to chase it with passion. You have to enter your own *Hot Pursuit*. When I think of a *Hot Pursuit*, I think of a relentless, obsessive, burning desire to fulfill a greater calling.

There are three distinct stages to the pursuing your dream with passion that we must all pass through in order to fully live our dreams and create an exceptional life. As you read my story, you'll learn how to assess which stage you're in and how you can make it to the next stage.

This may be *my* story, but I wrote this book for *you*. Is it time for *you* to discover and live your dream? If your heart is screaming, "YES!" as you read these words, then buckle up! Make today the day you decide to put *your* foot on the gas. I know from experience that the path will only become clear when you commit yourself to moving forward. This book is a tool to help you find the answers you need. It is my sincere and wholehearted hope that you find exactly what you're looking for.

Welcome, my friend! It's time to hit the road. I believe this journey can, and will, change your life!

Happy Travels!

Melissa V. West

"You have to dream before your dreams can come true."
A. P. J. Abdul Kalam

Introduction:
The Journey Starts Here

I'm so excited for you because you're moving closer to your dream. I know that your journey won't look like mine – our goals, paths, and destinations are different. Your roadmap will be as unique as you are. But there are three fundamental truths about dreams that are equally true for all of us, no matter where we're heading.

If you have ever seen one of those large "YOU ARE HERE" stars emblazoned on a map, then you know that when you see the star, it marks your starting point. The star gives you a way to orient yourself so you can begin to navigate the path to your destination. Just like the star orients you on the map, the following three truths can orient you on your journey.

Truth 1: Your Dream Is Tied To Your Purpose

Your dream is a manifestation of your purpose. You were created *with* and *for* a purpose and your dream is that purpose realized. When you were born, the seed of that purpose, was buried in your heart. It is critical that you pursue that purpose with a passion, because it belongs *exclusively* to you. You are the only person on Earth who can fulfill *your* purpose. Holocaust survivor, Victor Frankl, once said, *"Everyone has his own specific vocation or mission in life...Therein he cannot be replaced, nor can his life be repeated. Thus, everyone's task is as unique as is his specific opportunity to implement it."* You only get one shot at this life; don't waste the time you have. The world needs what you have to give!

Truth 2: Your Dream Is Bigger Than You

Your dream will *always* be bigger than you. Why? Because you have to grow *into* your dream. In fact, your personal growth is the catalyst for all the best things in life. NO matter what you want, if you focus on your own growth, then the world is your oyster. When you begin to succeed, greater opportunities come looking for you. Thankfully, no matter how much you grow, you can't outgrow your purpose. Therefore, "the chase" never ends. There is always more room for growth. Don't short-change your future by failing to invest in yourself. You are worth the investment!

Truth 3: Your Dream Is Filled With Energy

Over the years, I've had the privilege and honor to work with a number of amazing people. I'm blessed to call John C. Maxwell, the number one leadership expert in the world, both a mentor and a friend. After working closely with John for several years, I can tell you with all honesty that even though he is nearing 70 years old, he's just getting started. Do you know why he has so much energy? He's living his dream! In fact, his impact is growing exponentially because he keeps growing. As he grows, so do his dreams. Those dreams give him the energy of a 20-year-old. He claims he will never retire because his life's work feeds his passion and his dream. That's the kind of life I wish for – don't you? We deserve to live an exceptional life, filled with passion and energy! Let's not settle for a life that makes us want to hit the snooze button!

I wish I could tell you that your journey will be smooth sailing once you commit to the pursuit of your dreams. It will not. You are going to face difficulties and challenges and maybe even find a few roadblocks along the way. Realizing big, purpose-filled dreams is hard work! Each step of this journey helps us become the person we're meant to be and creates the internal resources we need to serve the people we're meant to serve. Make a habit of returning to these three truths. Keep them handy. Read them often and with intention. They will sustain you.

In fact, when pursuing your dreams, I highly I encourage you to surround yourself with uplifting words and inspiring thoughts. There's a poem I keep on my desk that reminds me to keep pushing myself and to never give up. It challenges me to continue pouring into people. It helps me stay focused as I cheer on my friends, colleagues, and clients. If these words speak to you, consider putting this poem in a place where you can refer to it easily. Meditate on its meaning. Let these words sink into your spirit. Reread them until you believe them with your whole heart. One of the most important things you can do right now is to focus on building your belief. Your belief will give you the energy you need on this journey.

Dreams Are Not Negotiable
Written by Adam Zane

Dreams. Our birthright.
They drive us, move us.
They fire us from the depths of our souls to create
the beautiful
the magnificent
the impossible.
They push you to go further.
And through our dreams, we can even change reality.

But know this my friend. Your dreams will be tested.
For the naysayers, the doubt instillers
and the fear-mongers await you at every corner.
Ready to push you down, to hold you back,
and no sooner as you get back to your feet
they will force you into a corner
silence your voice
and into your ear they will whisper...
"You're weak. You can't do it"

So hold your ground.
Don't demote your dreams to the past tense. Fight!
Fight for what is rightfully yours.
For you are the architect of your future,
and your dreams are the blueprint.
But fight not with bow and arrow, and sword and shield.
Fight the only way you know how,

fight with love.
For there is no power greater
and it is love that makes us who we are.

So should our eyes meet amidst the chaos and confu-
sion...
Allow yourself to shine.
For when I see you smile from beyond the ruins,
you give me permission to believe that I too can dream.
So be my muse and I will be your performer,
and together...
Let's dance across the rubble
Play music in the silence
Create art from beyond the void
And together we will be liberated of our fears.

Your dreams are not to be trifled with.
It is a contract you have signed
and it is not negotiable.
To dream is your birthright.
Live. Love. Dream.

Focus on the present, my friend. This moment. Right now. Take a few minutes to think about your dream. Whether you pursue it or not is up to you. And no matter what you decide – to stay stuck or move forward - you are making a choice. Never forget that the choices you make, *make you*.

Let this be the moment you fully embrace the future that belongs to you.

The Three Choices You Must Make to Begin Your Journey

Today, I choose to move forward. I will not wait another year, another day, or even another minute. My dream belongs to me. I believe that I was created and resourced to fulfill my purpose. From now on, I will enter into the pursuit of that dream. My dream belongs to me and I choose to claim it.

Today, I choose to embrace the journey. This is my life and it's my responsibility to live it to the fullest. I'm willing to jump in and embrace the unknown. I understand that the most important part of this journey is the process of *becoming*. I'm excited to discover the "new" me that I become as I follow my dream.

Today, I choose to step up. I accept that I will have to do things I've never done before. As scary and intimidating as it may be, I must fight for my dream, because no one else can fight for my dream but me. Even though this journey may be difficult and filled with trial and error, mistakes, and detours, I will carry on because my dream is worth it. And so am I. I commit to being the "architect of my future" because my purpose and future matter.

Congratulations! I'm proud of you for committing to your dream. You're on your way!

Happy Believing!

"Success is waking up in the morning and bouncing out of bed because there's something out there that you love to do, that you believe in, that you're good at — something that's bigger than you are, and you can hardly wait to get at it again."

Whit Hobbs

10 Ways to Help You Get the Most Out of This Book

1. **Focus on the most important thing.** If you want to get the most out of this book, then there is one thing that you absolutely MUST have – one non-negotiable ingredient that you need to succeed: DESIRE. Not an ordinary desire, either. You must be gripped by a *burning desire*, an unreasonable passion, for discovering and living your dream. Napoleon Hill, one of

the earliest writers of personal success litera-
ture, once said, *"Desire is the starting point of all
achievement, not a hope, not a wish, but a keen pul-
sating desire which transcends everything."* Unless
you have this one driving quality, then you can
read a thousand books on making your dreams
come true and nothing will come of it. How
can *you* develop this singular, focused desire?
By constantly reminding yourself *why* this
journey is important to you. By envisioning—
in detail—a future where you live your dream
life. By surrounding yourself with people who
support and encourage your dreams. By pouring into yourself every single day. Picture how
this journey can and will change your life.
Think on these things from sunrise to sunset.
Give yourself the gift of focused attention on
your dreams.

2. **Be fully present.** After you read each chapter
to get a big picture view of the content, slow
down and read the chapter again. You may be
tempted to rush on to the next chapter. Don't.
Remember, you're not reading for entertain-
ment; you are reading for transformation.
Transformation requires that you engage with
the content. Meditate on what you are reading.
What does it mean to you? Pay attention to the
passages that make your heart beat a little fast-

er. Why does it excite you? Be present with each idea. Ask yourself how and when you can apply each suggestion or idea into your personal and professional life. Focus your energy on getting the best *from yourself* as you read. Be an active participant in the reading process.

3. **Identify your stage.** There are three stages to pursuing your dream. As you read, identify where you are on your journey. Are you in Stage 1: *Discovering Your Dream*, Stage 2: *Breaking Through to Your Dream*, or Stage 3: *Living Your Dream*? No matter where you are, this book can help you move through the three stages. Let yourself experience this material, rather than simply read it. Hold each suggestion in your mind. Be honest with yourself. Most importantly, read with a commitment-focused mindset. This is your time, your dream, and your future. This book, and your experience as you read it, is an investment.

4. **Keep a pen handy while you read.** Underline the ideas that resonate with you. Note the ideas that encourage you to take action. I like to use the A-C-T acronym that I learned from John C. Maxwell. To use this method, you write an "A" next to every idea that you need to apply, a "C" next to ideas that challenge you

to change something, and a "T" next to the ideas you need to teach or share with others. This practice allows you to look for the best ideas. But more importantly, it helps you identify opportunities to take action so you can apply what you're learning.

5. **Journal your way to insight.** At the end of each chapter, you will find several questions to help you reflect as well as expand your thinking. Don't shortchange yourself by skipping those questions. I wrote these questions to help you gain the insight you want in order to develop the clarity you need. Give them your best thinking time. Even better, schedule your thinking time each day so you can return to the questions again and again as you read through the book. You may be surprised what you discover when you give yourself the time, space, and permission to explore your own thinking. Answers within you are waiting to be discovered.

6. **Follow reading with action.** George Bernard Shaw once remarked, *"If you teach a man anything, he will never learn."* He had a great point. We learn by doing, don't we? Learning is an active process; you will get the most benefit when you apply these ideas as quickly and as

frequently as possible. Repetition is your friend. If you truly want to see progress, then you need to get moving. That's why I named this book *Hot Pursuit*. You have to chase your dreams with passion, my friend! After all, action always precedes progress!

7. **Make your affirmations work for you.** I've had so many people tell me that affirmations don't work. Then, when I ask them when and how they use them, I realize that they've left out all three of the ingredients that make affirmations successful. First, you must say affirmations with conviction. Bathe the words in emotion. You must sound like you believe what you're saying. Secondly, you have to match your physiology with the emotion. Stand tall. Shoulders Back. Head straight. Palms up. When your body is awake and aware, your mind will follow suit. The third and final ingredient is repetition. You can't say an affirmation once and expect it to make a difference. You will find affirmation statements at the end of each chapter. I recommend that you write the affirmation on a sticky note and put copies of it where you will see it often – maybe on your bathroom mirror, the dashboard of your car, or on the door of your refrigerator. Also, don't be afraid to personalize the affirmations to suit you. There are lines un-

der each affirmation for this purpose. Feel free to add to the statement or change the wording to suit you and your goals. Make the most of the affirmations by adapting them to fit you and your needs.

8. **Review the signposts.** When you're traveling, road signs give you direction and guide you on your trip. You'll find that the Signposts for the Journey function in the same way. They summarize the main ideas clearly and concisely so you can re-visit the main concepts quickly and easily. You will also find them useful when you come back to the book for additional read-throughs. Don't skip over the signposts. They will help cement the big ideas in your mind.

9. **Give yourself grace and space.** This really *is* a journey. Don't expect to have immediate answers to your questions. Give yourself the space to explore and the grace to take chances, make mistakes, and be comfortable with "not knowing" all the answers. I'm sure you've heard that the journey is more important than the destination. It's the truth. Jump into this experience with passion, persistence, and patience. Each of these three qualities is incredibly important to have in your back pocket.

10. **Celebrate early and often. As you make progress in the pursuit of your dream, make sure you stop and celebrate.** I'm a firm believer in keeping a journal to record your successes. Write down your "wins" along the way. Each insight, each accomplishment, each step brings you closer to living your dream. Then, celebrate your progress. It's important to note that celebrating isn't just about woo-hooing and high-fiving. It goes deeper than that. Acknowledge the part of you that had to *think* differently and *do* differently in order to move forward. When we take the time to recognize even the small "wins" we've accomplished, we are feeding our belief and confidence in our abilities.

Stage 1:
Discovering Your Dream

Welcome! I'm so happy that you're joining me on this journey. Ten years ago, I made the decision to begin my *Hot Pursuit*. The decision wasn't an easy one. Though I could have settled for the good life I had at the time, I yearned for more. I suspect that you're reading this book because you feel the same way. Life is too short to live a small life, lacking passion and purpose. There are far too many people who settle; I'm so grateful that you aren't one of them. You will find that this journey is incredibly rewarding. I can't wait to see how your commitment benefits you and the world around you.

Happy Discovering!

Melissa V. West

Chapter 1:
Discover Your Dream
Destination

Let's travel back in time to the 1980s. I remember those days like they were yesterday: jamming to my Sony Walkman, singing along with Madonna and Michael Jackson on cassette tape. I was quite a sight - sporting mile-high bangs frozen in a perfect backward curl, held in place by an entire can of Aqua Net hairspray.

I could show you pictures of me back then that would make you laugh yourself hoarse.

In the 1980s, my family lived in a little blue house on the corner of Richard Street and Victoria Avenue in Waukesha, Wisconsin. We had a big, beautiful backyard where my sister and I climbed trees, played soccer, and hosted tea parties all summer. It was our favorite place in the world.

Later, as we got older, our parents decided that our backyard paradise was the perfect place to develop our work ethic, so they put my sister and I to work mowing, raking, and maintaining the yard. Around the same time, our parents began to give us routine lectures on the important things in life: getting good grades, going to a good college, getting a good job, and having a good family. They painted a very clear picture of what the "good" life looked like. *That picture became my guiding image for the next few years.*

I did exactly as they expected. I graduated from high school with honors and earned my bachelor's degree in Management Information Systems from the University of Wisconsin-Milwaukee. Then I landed a job as a web administrator for a fabulous company. For 27 years, this company had been rated number one in employee satisfaction. I had benefits, a solid income, and enjoyed working alongside my coworkers. The company was even paying for me to get my master's degree.

I put in my 40 or 50 hours per week and looked forward to the weekends. My friends, family, and colleagues did the same thing. And it was okay for a while...until it wasn't. I can't pinpoint the exact moment when I started to feel dissatisfied, but over time, a cloud began to form over me.

My mind started to wander at the office. Work began to feel like work. Meetings were an excuse to check out. At one point, I even found myself nodding off during a meeting. Knowing that this could get me in trouble, I recruited an elbow buddy.

Do you know what an elbow buddy is? An elbow buddy is someone who gives you a sharp elbow in the ribs and a "Wake up!" warning if you start to doze at an inopportune time.

One day, as I was sitting in a meeting, I realized how laughable my life had become. I felt as if I were living in a scene from "The Office." How had I reached the place where I needed an elbow buddy?

Suddenly, conscientious, hard-working Melissa became get-out-the door-as-fast-as-you-can-at-quitting-time Melissa. I had my running shoes laced up at 4:55 so I could make a break for the parking lot the second that 5:00 p.m. rolled around. I started counting the days or weeks until the next major escape from work: When was the next holiday? How long would it be until my next vacation day? I was surviving one day to the next and the weekend couldn't come fast enough.

Strangely, although it sounds like it, I didn't hate my job. But I felt like a robot. There was no joy, no passion, and no life in what I was doing. And if you know me today, you know that I am *full of life, passion, and joy*!

I had what success was supposed to look like, but it didn't feel right to me. Why? Looking back, I realize that there was one critical piece missing.

I had the life my parents wanted for me, not the life I wanted for myself. There was nothing wrong with the life they wanted for me. It just wasn't the right fit.

Now I realize that no one had ever asked me what I wanted. Not my counselor, not my parents, not even me! My life was a mismatch because I allowed someone else to define my destination. I was living someone else's dream for me.

Here's the thing: although I had to leave my job to follow my dreams, you may be on a very different path. Perhaps your dream is to mentor leaders in your current organization, or start a church, or be a better parent or spouse. Maybe you want to expand your business, launch a new product, or write a book. No matter what your greater purpose is, know this:

> *You can't achieve success until you define it for yourself.*

One of the greatest threats to your dream is your preconceived, unquestioned ideas about success. I would venture to guess that you're carrying around some expectations that have been placed upon you – either by your teachers, your parents, your community, or even your spouse.

Perhaps it's time to reevaluate what you believe. If you have the wrong formula for success, you'll *never* get the results you want. It's that simple.

> *One of the greatest threats to your dream is your preconceived, unquestioned ideas about success.*

A New Definition of Success

I love, love, love life and business coach, Marie Forleo. She's had a tremendous impact on my perception of life and business. Recently, I was listening to one of her "Q and A Tuesday" videos where she gave three tips for developing your own definition of success.

First, Forleo said that you have to remember that "your work does not equal your worth." I don't know how that sits with you, but it feels both obvious and counterintuitive to me. Sure, I realize that my true, authentic, lasting worth is in who I am, but I admit that I've struggled with associating my work with my worth. I'm passionate about what I do. I believe my work makes a difference. I believe that it is a worthy pursuit. But ultimately, Forleo is right. Our work and worth are not the same thing. Give yourself some slack. Your work matters, but your worth is a given.

Secondly, she said that the best way to get clarity is to begin with the end in mind. Forleo described the following exercise: "Imagine it's your last day on Earth. Think back on your journey." Then answer a series of questions such as, "What kind of memories do you want to have? What kind of adventures will you have taken? Are there certain places you went, friends you made, and things you did with them?" That's great advice. But it's not enough to imagine these things. You need to write them down. We create by first articulating what we want. Journaling can help you gain the clarity and perspective you need on your journey.

Finally, Forleo suggested that you, "Flesh out the details" and ask, "What would make you feel accomplished?" I tend to think of this question in terms of creating a day-to-day sense of accomplishment. What if you focused less on creating a successful life, and more on creating a successful day? After all, a successful life is nothing more than a series of successful days. What makes one day more successful than another?[1]

These questions may be difficult to answer, but I promise you, they're worthwhile. Dig in and ask yourself the tough questions. Challenge yourself to reevaluate the decisions you've made in the past. Think about how your definition of success needs to change. The more you know, the further you can go.

Remember, an exceptional life is a well-examined life.

Happy Defining!

---

[1] Forleo, Marie. "How To Define Success For Yourself, No Matter What The World Says." Marie Forleo. Accessed February 22, 2016. http://www.marieforleo.com/2015/03/definition-of-success/.

Journal for the Journey

1. Project yourself to the end of your life. Now look backward in time. Imagine what your best possible life would have looked like. What kind of memories do you have? Which places have you visited? How have you spent your time? How do you know that you were successful? What gives you the greatest sense of fulfillment? When did you feel the happiest?

_____

_____

_____

_____

2. Now, think about how your best moments look right now. What makes you feel a sense of accomplishment? What makes you come alive? When do you feel happiest? When do you feel full of passion and energy?

_____

_____

_____

_____

3. How do you define success *for yourself*?

_____

_____

_____

_____

4. How does your current life (and lifestyle) align with your definition?

_____

_____

_____

_____

5. What is your biggest insight from this activity? How does it impact your view of yourself and your future?

_____

_____

_____

_____

"Success is liking who you are, liking what you do, and liking how you do it."

Maya Angelou

Affirmation

Today, I choose to reevaluate my definition of success. I understand that my goals will align with my highest priorities. I know that a fulfilling future is the result of the day-to-day work that creates a well-lived life. I embrace this journey and the self-examination that makes it possible. I believe that the clarity I'm seeking already exists within me. My commitment to this experience will allow me to see what is waiting to be discovered.

Signposts for the Journey

1. When you begin to find yourself *checking out* at work, at home, or with friends, it's time to *check in* with yourself.

2. You can't achieve success until you define it for yourself.

3. An exceptional life is a well-examined life.

4. Your work and your worth are not the same.

5. A successful life is nothing more than a series of successful days.

"When you have the courage to question what you're doing and, more importantly, why you're doing it — you stay on your edge of innovation, truth and lasting fulfillment."

Marie Forleo

Chapter 2:
Discover Your Dream's Purpose

Being bored and unhappy didn't sit well with me. But I didn't know what to do about the growing sense of dissatisfaction that was burning a hole in the pit of my stomach. I became fixated on the idea that my life was *meant* to be bigger and better.

Since I was *completely* lost, I did what every confused, misguided person does. I took up skydiving.

Depending on your personality, that may sound awesome or crazy. I don't know how to explain it, but at the time it felt right to me. I was tired of being a robot. I wanted to FEEL again, and there's nothing like throwing yourself out of a perfectly good plane to make you feel again, even if all you feel is terror!

I loved the addictive rush I got from skydiving. Those moments when I was racing toward the ground, with my heart in my throat and the wind roaring in my ears, were incredible. I was absolutely, one hundred percent in the moment. Take a second and imagine me, dropping through the air with the biggest, cheesiest, most ridiculous ear-to-ear smile. Skydiving made me happy from the top of my head to the tips of my toes.

The downside, unfortunately, was that though I loved skydiving, my bank account hated it. And honestly, even though it made me happy, the happiness was short-lived. Once I was back on solid ground, my dissatisfaction returned with a vengeance.

Looking back, I know why my happiness was fleeting. I was searching for answers, but what I found was an adrenaline rush. More than anything, I wanted to grow and improve. I craved transformation. For me, there was no room for growth in skydiving. I wasn't motivated to get certified to jump solo or to complete the training to become an instructor. It was a one-sided love affair: I loved skydiving and skydiving loved my money. We parted ways amicably.

Undeterred, when the voice in my head started asking, "Okay, what's next?" I already had an answer: running marathons. That was it! I mean, that's what everyone does, right? If you don't know what you want to be when you grow up, you lace up your shoes and run your way to blisters….and hopefully, self-awareness.

Until I began running marathons, I'd never been a runner. But I've also never been one to let little things – like a lack of skill, training, and athleticism – stop me. I threw myself into the sport with complete abandon, running in the evenings and on the weekends. I trained hour after hour, pushing my body and mind past every limit I thought I had. I've got to tell you, there's something beautiful that happens when your mind is forced to stretch in order to push your body. I had to grow mentally and physically to keep going.

But, once again, the rush didn't last. By the time I got to my second marathon, the glow had worn off and I was left with aching legs and oozing blisters. As I sat there one day, treating my feet after a race, I had an "aha!" moment. I thought, "All right, so I'm jumping out of airplanes and I'm running marathons and it's fun. It's really fun. But wait a minute, I don't have a problem with my hobbies or social life: I have a problem with my career. *So what am I doing?* Why am I jumping out of airplanes and running marathons? This isn't getting me any closer to finding the road I'm supposed to be on."

Have you ever done that? Have you ever put all your time, energy, and effort into something only to realize that no matter how hard you try, you're never going to get any closer to finding the answer because *you've been asking the wrong question all along?*

> **I was looking for fun when I should have been looking for meaning.**

I wanted a reason to get up each morning. I needed to believe that I was contributing to the world in a way that mattered. I was tired of feeling empty. That's why it was so tempting to jump into activities that made me feel a sense of satisfaction, even if it was short-lived. I needed more. As a result, I became a victim of "shiny object syndrome."

If you aren't familiar with *shiny object syndrome,* it is simply an overwhelming attraction to every new idea that comes your way. Each idea seems to capture your attention and distract you from the bigger picture. Instead of staying focused on your goals, you chase every "shiny object" that catches your eye. I happen to be an *expert* at finding shiny objects to chase. Every time I allowed myself to get distracted, I wasted precious time.

What I've learned through this process is that our dreams are a catalyst. As we chase them, they help us discover our purpose. I believe that we are all here for a reason. Our dreams guide and direct our steps as we discover the bigger *why* behind our goals and aspirations.

But without a clear dream guiding our way, we can start to feel lost. If you're anything like me, you hate feeling lost.

That's exactly how I felt. I sensed that I had a bigger purpose, but I had no clue how to discover it. My purpose seemed sneaky and elusive. Finding it felt a little like locating my car keys when I'm in a hurry. The bottom of my purse is dark and cluttered and the mess makes it harder to find what I'm looking for. Though I *know* my keys are there, I can't see them. The same was true with my purpose. I knew I had one, but I couldn't seem to find it.

Though I may have felt a little lost, I had two things going for me: dogged determination and a habit of reflection. I kept seeking answers both inside and outside of myself. That experience, missteps and all, was a valuable process. I learned, in the midst of chasing every shiny object, to ask myself an important question: Am I chasing the right thing?

If my answer was "no," then I had to keep looking.

Are you chasing the right things, my friend? If your answer is "no," then take my word for it: You have to keep looking! Search until you find the *right* thing. Explore with wild abandon. Hunt high and low until you find the answers you need. Your eager willingness to keep exploring is a critical component of your pursuit. As Jack London said, *"You can't wait for inspiration. You have to go after it with a club."*

It may take a while to discover your purpose, but you move closer every time you take a step forward. I'm proud of you for taking the time to invest in yourself and discover your next steps!

Happy Hunting!

Watch Out, I've Gone Purpose-Huntin'

When I think about hunting for your purpose, I get the hilarious image of the Looney Tunes cartoon character, Yosemite Sam, in my head. Do you remember him? Yosemite Sam was the rabbit-hating, gun-slinging, arch enemy of Bugs Bunny. He had a giant red mustache and a hair-trigger temper. With his unforgettable exaggerated drawl he'd say things like, "Any one of you lily-livered, bow-legged varmints care to slap leather with me?"

He was funny...and relentless. Yosemite Sam never gave up on the hunt for Bugs Bunny. That's how you have to be on this journey – relentless and a bit obsessive. Don't wait until you have all the answers. This is one of the most important pieces of advice I can give you – Give yourself permission to figure things out as you go. Listen to me carefully. *It's completely okay to not know what you're doing.* In fact, it's normal! This may sound strange, but the discomfort you feel is actually a gift. Be thankful for it. It exists to push you toward who you were meant to be.

In his book, *The Art of Work²*, writer, Jeff Goins, says, *"You don't 'just know' what your calling is. You must listen for clues along the way, discovering what your life can tell you. Awareness comes with practice."* Did you know that the original meaning of the word *discover* was to uncover or unveil? That's

---

² Goins, Jeff. *The Art of Work: A Proven Path to Discovering What You Were Meant to Do.* Thomas Nelson. Available on Amazon at http://amzn.com/0718022076

why I love the word 'discover' in Goins' quote. He says you must *uncover or unveil* what your life has to tell you. This is the awesome thing: You can't uncover something unless it was there all along! Whether you know it or not, your purpose exists. It's there, burning inside of you. You wouldn't be reading this book if that weren't true. You are exactly where you are supposed to be, doing exactly what you are supposed to be doing.

> *The gap between experience and insight is bridged by self-awareness.*

Keep exploring, but also keep this in mind: the gap between experience and insight is bridged by self-awareness. It's not enough to skydive and run marathons. Exploration without reflection may be fun, but it won't get you closer to your bigger why. These three tips will help you bridge the gap.

1. Let your curiosity be your guide; it will help you uncover your purpose.

2. Release yourself from judgment. This is a personal journey, so give yourself permission to explore with abandon.

3. Invest in the process. Experience without awareness is useless. Spend time in reflection and journal your way to insight.

Journal for the Journey

1. When do you feel most curious and intrigued?

_____

_____

_____

_____

2. What captures your attention when you lose track of time?

_____

_____

_____

_____

3. What do you love to read in your spare time?

_____

_____

_____

_____

4. Is there anything you've always wanted to try, but haven't?

_____

_____

_____

_____

5. In which area of your business (or life) do you feel compelled to solve problems?

_____

_____

_____

_____

6. If you had to pick out two things you could do to move you forward on this journey, what would they be?

_____

_____

_____

_____

7. What can you commit to do or accomplish this week?

_____

_____

_____

_____

*"If you never chase your dreams,
you will never catch them."*

Unknown

Affirmation

I believe that my dream exists to inspire and challenge me. I have a purpose. Because I am the only person that can fulfill that purpose, I choose to relentlessly chase my dream until I "uncover it." From this point on, I see myself as an explorer on a mission. I choose to embrace new experiences because they will give me insight and awareness. I value my growth and my future; therefore, I commit myself to this journey.

Signposts for the Journey

Your dreams are meant for more than inspiration; they are meant to guide you to your purpose.

1. It's normal to not know what you are doing. Persist anyway.

2. Exploration without reflection may be fun, but it won't get you closer to your dream or help you get clarity on your purpose.

3. Release yourself from judgment. Keep trying things on until you find the right fit.

4. Your purpose exists; it's just waiting for you to discover it.

"Before the plan, there is an idea. Before the idea, there is a purpose. Before the purpose, there is your spirit...aching to express itself."

Paresh Shah

Chapter 3:
Discover Your Dream GPS

It's easier to jump into distractions than it is to dive into self-discovery. Self-discovery takes work while fun distractions are...well...fun. And, as you can tell from my skydiving and marathon adventures, I'm a sucker for fun! But it didn't take long for me to realize something critical to this journey. Distractions are thieves. They will steal your focus if you let them.

I remember telling myself, *"Focus, Melissa, focus. Quit playing around. It's time to find answers and clarity in your career."*

It was January 2007 and I had come home from a long day at work, kicked off my shoes, and turned on the television. Oprah Winfrey had a panel of guests on her show, and the topic for the day was *potential*. The guests were discussing the fact that we can use our unlimited potential to improve every area of our lives.

Unlimited potential? I have the power to create what I want in my life? Improvement is just a decision away? It blew my mind. I swear to you, those people on television were speaking directly TO ME. Suddenly, I wasn't tired anymore. My heart was racing. I felt like someone had turned up the heat in my condo. I was breathing hard and fast. I was literally on the edge of my seat, thinking, "Whoa. I want that. Unlimited potential. The power to create what I want. Yes. That's it!"

It wasn't the first time I'd heard that message, but on that particular day, it hit me like a ton of bricks. Who knew I'd find the answer to life's burning questions on the "Oprah Winfrey Show"?

I guess you just never know where inspiration will strike!

The interesting thing is that all I had was one single moment of insight. It wasn't as if a gold brick road appeared to mark my path. I didn't get a note on the table or a phone call from God. I didn't receive a list of detailed instructions. There was simply a light bulb that went off in my mind, followed by one pulsing thought that kept repeating itself: *This is right.* The moment was both ordinary and magical at the same time.

For most of us, we get a clue to our dream here and an insight there. We find one answer and all it leads us to is the next answer. All I could think at the time was, "Hallelujah! I've finally found a clue!"

Though I didn't understand the significance when I was watching Oprah talk about potential, it *was* a defining moment. What I've discovered, after coaching thousands of people, is that we each have these moments, moments when the haze lifts and things suddenly become clear. Every client I've had, without exception, has had this experience.

Someday, somewhere, you will have your own Oprah experience. There will be a moment when something speaks to you, calls you, and hits you upside the head. Is it possible to miss your defining moment? Absolutely. Many people pass these experiences by, without a second thought. Unknowing, they fail to recognize the physical and emotional sensations that signal their potentially life-changing insight.

I've often wondered if there were signs I missed before that pivotal day, and I'm convinced that there were. I believe we get clues to our dreams from a very young age, but if we don't know what we're looking for, we miss them. Thankfully, our dreams are persistent. Even if you once had a dream, but gave up on it somewhere along the way, I can promise you this: Your dream hasn't given up on you. Somewhere deep inside, it's still calling to you.

The question isn't whether or not this will happen to you. The question is – *when* your time comes, will you be paying attention? Will you reach into yourself and find the courage to chase your passion?

When that moment came for me, I had a tremendous sense of urgency. I love how John C. Maxwell describes these experiences. He says that when he senses opportunity, he dives right in. He doesn't dip his toe in the water, test the temperature, or look to see if anyone else is in the water. He dives.

The people on that episode of "The Oprah Winfrey Show" inspired something in me that I couldn't turn off. I dove into personal and professional development with a passion that's hard to describe. From that moment on, I was as relentless and obsessive as Yosemite Sam, reading anything

I could get my hands on about leadership, psychology, mindset, goal setting, and attitude. As Les Brown would say, "I was HUUUUUNGRY!"

After a few months of reading and researching, I came across a website describing a coaching certification program. By that point, I knew without question that personal growth was part of my future. The website outlined a certification program that would allow me to become a life and business coach. It explained that there were people out there, waiting for me to help them grow into their potential. Once again, the words were speaking directly to my heart. My body went on high alert. Before I'd read halfway down the page, I was ALL IN. I may not have known what I was looking for before that particular moment, but when I found that program, I *knew* it was right.

The question is – when your time comes, will you be paying attention?

Looking back, I realize that even though I loved skydiving and running marathons, they weren't what I was put on this earth to do. They were hobbies, not dreams. Committing to this program, on the other hand, was the first step on my journey. I knew it as sure as I knew my own name.

T.D. Jakes[3] calls this finding our "internal heartbeat." According to him, our ability to recognize when we're on the right path (or the wrong one) is a learned skill. He says that, "It can be hard at first to identify that internal heartbeat, but recognizing it determines what will give you fulfillment and gratification. Think of it as an inward applause for every moment when you feel in harmony with yourself, and when you hear it – be it loud and clear or soft and slightly muffled – you'll know exactly what it is and what you're meant to do."

"Inward applause" perfectly describes what I felt every time I discovered a new step. For many of my clients, these moments come and go for different reasons. They might be waiting until the timing is right, until there's money is in the bank, or until the kids are grown. While they are waiting for their specific obstacle to pass, their dream is passing, too.

---

[3] "Bishop T.D. Jakes: 4 Mistakes That Keep You from Finding Your Purpose." Oprah.com. http://www.oprah.com/oprahs-lifeclass/TD-Jakes-4-Mistakes-That-Keep-You-from-Finding-Your-Purpose.

If you are serious about getting clarity about your dream, then *you* have to take charge of your role in this journey. Dive in. Search relentlessly for that moment of insight when you know – *this is right.* Then go for it!

> **Your internal heartbeat is your dream GPS.**
> **It will guide you if you listen.**

There is nothing more important on this journey than your ability to listen to yourself. Malcolm Gladwell says that, *"Insight is not a lightbulb that goes off inside our heads. It is a flickering candle that can easily be snuffed out."* Gladwell is right when he says that your defining moments can be snuffed out. They can sneak past you without warning. But if you are paying attention, your body will sound the alarm and your internal heartbeat will send you the message: *This is right.*

Reflection is arguably the most important habit you can develop. Take time to think and give yourself the space to listen. I realize that the busyness of our lives doesn't leave much time for reflection, but you have to *make* time. There is no other way to find the answers you're seeking.

And if insight approaches on tiptoe, as quiet as a mouse, don't lose heart. Your "internal heartbeat" will get louder and stronger the more you listen for it.

Happy Listening!

Follow the Crumbs

Maybe I'm a romantic, but I tend to think that these moments are actually Destiny setting crumbs in front of me, marking the path to my future. Ultimately, I'm in charge of finding (or ignoring) the crumbs. Every *"this is right"* moment is a crumb that gets me closer to my dream and my personal destiny.

I hope that this book is one of the crumbs that Destiny has set before you. There's no greater joy than seeing people begin to pick up the crumbs that lead to the future of their dreams. I believe that your pursuit is simply a big series of little defining moments. Your ability to identify them in real time can be the difference between chasing your dreams and living them. Develop habits that allow you to be more present. Pay attention to the physiological signals that your body sends you. There's a mountain of good reading material on how to become more mindful and self-aware. Start reading. (Or listen – I love audio books, too!) I believe these habits can greatly increase your ability to recognize life-changing flashes of insight when they happen.

Another way to deepen your awareness is to interview other people who are living their dreams. I encourage you to seek out someone this week. Talk to them about how they got where they are. Ask them how *they* identified their defining moments. Try to understand the characteristics that gave them the courage to act when their next step becomes clear. Find out how their willingness to take action has impacted their life. My bet is that they will be more than happy to share the "crumbs" that they found and followed on their path.

Journal for the Journey

1. Think of a positive defining moment from your past. Did you sense that it was a defining moment at the time? Looking back, were there any signals that it was a defining moment?

_____

_____

_____

_____

2. What decision did you have to make? Why was it difficult?

_____

_____

_____

_____

3. When you were able to get clear about what you should do, how did you know it was the right next step?

_____

_____

_____

_____

4. What gave you the courage to act in that situation?

_____

_____

_____

_____

5. Why do you think you were able to get clarity in that particular situation?

_____

_____

_____

_____

6. What lesson/learning could you apply from that situation as you continue to pursue your dreams?

_____

_____

_____

_____

"When you reach the end of what you should know, you will be at the beginning of what you should sense."
Khalil Gibran

Affirmation

I believe in the power of my dreams. From this moment forward, I choose to pay attention to the signals that my body and heart are sending me. I understand that I must actively participate in this journey, and I commit to looking for and following the crumbs that Destiny has left in my path. I have the courage and self-awareness to recognize the defining moments in my life.

Signposts for the Journey

1. Distractions are thieves. They will steal your focus if you let them.

2. Your ability to identify defining moments in real time can make the difference between chasing and living your dreams.

3. Your internal heartbeat is your dream GPS. It will guide you if you listen.

4. Pay attention to the physiological signals that your body sends you; those signals are like a neon sign pointing the way.

5. It is not enough to see the crumbs: you must follow them.

"You have to participate relentlessly in the manifestation of your own blessings."

Elizabeth Gilbert

Stage 2: Breaking Through To Your Dream

The Three Tests You Must Pass to Make Your Dream a Reality

Congratulations! You are on your way. The world needs people who are eager and willing to do the hard work of becoming the best version of themselves. I'm so glad you are one of those people!

If you feel like you are on the right path (even if your vision is hazy), then you are ready to enter Stage 2: *Breaking Through to Your Dream.*

If not, take heart and keep exploring. The great gift of insight comes through action. Your direction will become clear with time.

If you're ready to take it to the next level, here's a heads up. You are going to find roadblocks in your path. This is one of the biggest challenges in Stage 2. The roadblocks are going to slow you down and will likely frustrate you. It's okay. After coaching thousands of people on this journey, I can honestly say - this happens to everyone.

Here's the good news – the roadblocks don't exist to stop you from going where you are meant to go. They have a purpose. They are meant to teach you, test you, and most importantly, guide you on your journey. With the right perspective and attitude, these roadblocks will serve your highest good by helping you develop your perseverance, commitment, and love for the place you are going.

Focus on your gift of growth in this stage. Every roadblock gets you closer to your dream. You get to choose whether you see those roadblocks as an obstacle or a blessing. Choose to be blessed.

As you break through them one by one, they will increase your belief in yourself and your vision.

Happy Breaking Through!

Melissa V. West

Chapter 4:
Passing the Commitment Test

As I mentioned in Chapter 3, one of the biggest misconceptions about dream discovery is that there's a single lightbulb moment when the path forward becomes crystal clear and there's only smooth sailing from that point on. Oh, how I wish that were true!

Your moment of clarity, powerful though it may be, is just the beginning.

When I said "yes" to my dream, I meant it. But I had a problem.

The coaching program of my dreams cost big money: $16,000. Yes. Sixteen. Thousand. Dollars.

Do you know how much money I had when I started my business?

I was $16,000 in the hole.

That's right. Budget-conscious, count-every-penny Melissa took out a loan to cover the entire amount.

Are you wondering why in the world I would do that? Well, I wondered the same thing. All I know is that I made the choice to act based on the tiny bit of faith I had at the time. It wasn't an easy decision for me. It was painful. In fact, I spent three weeks looking at the details of the program. I weighed and balanced every cost and benefit. I went back and forth in my head a dozen times. I ran the numbers and knew that it might take years to pay off the debt. I prayed on it hoping God would give me the immediate answer I was looking for!

But a desperate soul can also be a daring soul. And I was desperate. I'd spent my whole life on a path I'd never really wanted to go down. I may have been *terrified* of going into debt, but I was *more terrified* of the future I was heading toward. Spending the money was risky, but I had no other choice. Once again, I decided to dive in. Head first. No safety net.

Since that day, I've had numerous people ask me how I made that kind of commitment when I still felt like I was wandering in the dark. I wish I could give them an impressive answer, but I simply *made a decision*. I knew that if I didn't pursue the program, I was going to regret it. I can't tell you why that particular certification program spoke to me so deeply. It just did. If you believe in God, or fate, or intuition, you will understand why it felt like something bigger than me was directing my steps.

I made a leap of faith. Now, let me stop for a minute to tell you that I love it when people say they took *a leap of faith*. It's a powerful statement. As a professional coach, I hear many people tell me that they have faith. Faith that it will all work out. Faith that they'll find answers. Faith in something bigger than them. But when it comes to leaping - that's another story. They may have faith, but they're unwilling to act on it.

> *People get stuck because they wait for their circumstances to change instead of choosing to change their circumstances.*

My entire life is built around helping people identify their dream and then take steps in that direction, so I'm fascinated by what makes some people wait while others leap. What I've found is that many people get stuck in this stage. They wait for their circumstances to change instead of choosing to change their circumstances.

As a result, they treat their dream like a hobby. But it's impossible to achieve dream-level results with hobby-level effort. And a dream with half-hearted effort – a dream without sacrifice – is a hobby.

I don't know what your dream will require of you, but I know that all dreams come with a price. Though my initial sacrifice was financial, yours may be different. Yours may require a sacrifice of time, energy, or focus. I may be sharing these tests through the lens of my story, but keep this in mind: The three tests apply to *every* journey. Your dream may look nothing like mine. It may be more leadership, family, or faith-focused. Or it may be something entirely unique to you. It doesn't matter. These tests are part of the journey.

No matter what the sacrifice looks like, you can't move forward without *moving forward*. Change can't happen if we are rooted in one spot. The Commitment Test will require you to do something you've never done before. It will force you to act. To say yes. To get up early. To pay the fee. To create a team. To work on the relationship. To share your vision. To launch the product. To go to the gym. To go back to the drawing board. To create something new.

Ultimately, the Commitment Test is all about you making an intentional choice when the time comes. But if you get to this Stage and are willing to make that choice, then I have good news for you. One of the biggest and most wonderful gifts you receive from this experience starts here, at this point where opportunity meets sacrifice. Why? Because sacrifice requires commitment. You won't pay a price for something you don't believe in – for something that doesn't speak to your heart.

This is a big deal. Don't underestimate the *value* of this step.

Each sacrifice you make builds your belief.

That's a powerful statement. Sacrifice builds belief. Sit with that thought for a minute. Let it bounce around inside you.

This is why the Commitment Test is important. Think of it like this: Imagine that you have a belief bank account. Every time you make a sacrifice in the pursuit of your dream, you make a deposit in your belief account. If you keep making deposits, your balance grows. Each sacrifice is an opportunity to build your account balance. Over time, you'll build your belief to the point that it will be difficult to shake!

When I started this journey, all I had was a *tiny seed of belief*. If that's all you have as well, then be encouraged. That's all you need!

With every commitment and sacrifice, my belief grew. I wish I'd known that those moments of fear had a purpose. You see, those choices moved me closer to my dream. They were valuable because they were building *me*! This is the second great payoff of The Commitment Test.

Every time you choose to move forward, you come closer to the person who was made to live your dream and fulfill your purpose. *Though we are all works in progress, this is a critical point. Your journey is as much about who you become as what you do.*

Each test is positive and purposeful. These tests exist to teach, guide, and shape you on your journey. With the right perspective and attitude, each one will serve your highest good. They will not only help you build your belief account but they will build you, too!

Happy Committing!

4 Tips to Help You Take Your Own Leap of Faith

I wish I could sit with you and learn the details of your dream. I want to understand what's in your heart as well as what keeps you up at night. Since we can't be together in person as you're reading these words, please imagine me beside you. If you are plagued by doubts and fears, know that it's okay to be scared. Let me be the first to tell you, *what you're feeling is normal.* If it were easy to achieve our dreams, then we'd have a world full of happy, fulfilled people, wouldn't we?

But sadly, we don't live in that world. Dream chasing is sometimes hard, nerve-wracking work. Just in case you think that I had resources of courage that you don't, let me assure you that I was not any braver than you, my friend. I was terrified. But I had this tiny little flicker of hope in my heart and I chose to focus all my energy on that. I'm betting that down deep inside, you have some hope flickering inside you, too.

Use that little flicker to help you make the leap. Remember, faith is important, but it's the leap that moves you forward. Business consultant, Stay Michelle, writes about this idea on her website, mindbodygreen.com. There, she offers several excellent tips for developing the "joyful courage" it takes to go for it. She says you must,

1. Listen to the voice in your head. Your inner voice has some very important things to say. Think of it as a more evolved version of yourself saying, "Hey Lady [or Man,] check this out!" In today's world where we tend to look for outsiders for advice, we often ignore our inner voice. When you have a gut instinct about something, trust it and follow it.

2. Practice daily self-care. When we take the road less traveled, it can be stressful. This is why it's so important to stop, breathe, and nourish your body and soul in whatever way works for you.

3. Replace fear of the unknown with a sense of desire for what's to come. Being in the unknown can be scary, but try to replace your fear with desire for the passion you are pursuing. Take 5-10 minutes every day and visualize it. What does it look like? What does it feel like? Who is around you? When you can stay in that beautiful energetic state that is desire, you are more likely to cultivate your passion with ease.

4. Quit comparing yourself to others around you. It's easy to get wrapped up in timelines and compare yourself to what your peers have already cultivated. Everyone has their own respective journey of what they're manifesting in life. Focus on your desires, and trust that if you pay attention to what you want, it will happen exactly as it's supposed to.[4]

The good news about leaping is that it gets easier with practice. Take care of yourself and build your belief account. It's time to take a leap!

"The brick walls are there for a reason. The brick walls are not there to keep us out. The brick walls are there to give us a chance to show how badly we want something."

Randy Pausch, *The Last Lecture*

---

[4] Michelle, Stacy. "7 Tips For Anyone About To Take A Leap Of Faith." Mindbodygreen. June 6, 2014. http://www.mindbodygreen.com/0-13997/7-tips-for-anyone-about-to-take-a-leap-of-faith.html.

Journal for the Journey

1. Why do you feel compelled to pursue your dreams right *now*?

_____

_____

_____

_____

2. Do you believe that *who you become* has an impact on your outcome? Why or why not?

_____

_____

_____

_____

3. Have you had a *"this is right"* moment on your journey so far? If so, what did you learn about yourself?

_____

_____

_____

_____

4. Is there a trade-off that you could make right now that would move you closer to your dream? What would the benefit be if you were to make the trade-off?

_____

_____

_____

_____

5. How can you reframe your commitments in a way that allows you to see the opportunity even in the midst of uncertainty?

_____

_____

_____

_____

Affirmation

Every step I take gets me closer to my dream. I understand that this dream will require something of me. I accept that I have to grow in order to live my dream and that each sacrifice is an invitation to grow. I am bold and courageous. I embrace this part of the journey and choose to make every sacrifice intentional and purpose-filled.

Chapter 5:
Passing the Courage Test

A week after I signed my life away, Ronald, my UPS guy, showed up on my doorstep. He had a truck full of coaching material to deliver, and those boxes had my name on them. As he stacked the boxes in the corner of my living room, I got giddier by the second. When he left, I stood there and stared. Those boring, unassuming boxes held *my future.*

You'd think I would've ripped right in, wouldn't you? I mean, this was it! But that's not what I did. Nope. Not me. Sure and certain Melissa decided to have a meltdown instead. My excitement evaporated as I stared at that mountain of boxes. It was overwhelming.

So I didn't open them on the first day. Or the second. Then two days turned into two weeks. And two weeks turned into two months. Every morning, I walked past those boxes on my way to the job I didn't want. Every day, I'd tell myself that I would open those boxes after work. But I didn't. Every evening, I came home, sat on the same couch where my dream had first become clear, and watched television.

And every evening those boxes seemed to mock me. "When, Melissa? When are you going to start? Next month? Next year? Why kid yourself?" And every night I would argue, "That's not true. What do you want from me? I worked all day. I'll open you up this weekend!"

Now, aside from sounding a bit crazy, I was frustrated. I felt guilty about avoiding those boxes because I knew (and I knew that I knew) that they were my next step. So, why in the world didn't I open them?

Looking back, I realize I was in neutral. All I had to do was shift into gear, but I chose to sit there, idling. I see the same pattern with my clients today. Can you relate? Have you ever stalled out after making an investment? I bet you have. Maybe it was a gym membership that you purchased, but then only used twice. Or maybe it is the treadmill in the corner of your bedroom that masquerades as a clothes hanger. If you're like me, you buy books that never get read and programs that never get used. We buy this stuff with the full intention of using it, but it gets put on a shelf or stored out of the way and then it just....sits there. Why? *Because our investment in the exercise equipment, program, or book outweighed our willingness to actually use them.*

I'd rather not admit it, but I argued with myself over those unopened boxes for four months. Four months! Day after day, those boxes sat in the corner of my living room and taunted me. I was so busy letting those boxes represent my fear that they *couldn't* represent my future.

In the absence of intentional focus, your mind will make up any story that it wants. My mind decided that those boxes represented doubt and instability. I mean, who wants to open boxes that scare you all the way down to your toes? While I was arguing with those boxes, they were saying really nasty things to me. Things like, "What do you think you are doing? Who in the world would hire you? And why would you risk everything? You have a house, a car, a good job. What more do you want? You don't know what you're getting yourself into. Your life is good and you're going to jump into a business? How? Life is about to get really, really bumpy. Get ready."

That wasn't the only message I heard from the boxes. They'd also rant, "Are you crazy? Why did you risk everything? Do you even know how much it costs to run a business? Sixteen thousand dollars is just the beginning. Financial security? Good luck with that! You're going to go broke!"

It was hard to argue with those statements, because there was truth in them. I *was scared* of starting a business. I *didn't know* what I was doing. I *couldn't answer* the question, "How?"

Those boxes reinforced every one of my limiting beliefs. I had no network and no business plan. I had no idea who was going to hire me. I didn't know how to describe my services even if someone had asked. I had no idea how to begin or what to charge. In my mind, I'd failed and I hadn't even started.

Those boxes screamed uncertainty. So, they sat there and gathered dust.

By the end of month four, I was feeling pretty defeated. One day, when looking at the calendar, I realized that the final phase of my coaching program was approaching quickly. I was supposed to fly to Florida to participate in a live training event. Obviously, I was totally unprepared. I debated about going because I had no desire to look as ignorant as I clearly was. But even though a part of me feared getting "found out," I couldn't resist the idea of attending a big event at a fancy hotel. I couldn't wait to meet new people, get some sun, and have some fun. If I'd learned anything from my skydiving and marathon days, it was that my desire for fun often outweighs my fear!

I packed my bags and decided to show up – to be fully present – even though I was nervous and uncertain. I was assigned to a table and made friends quickly. I soaked in every second. I listened and laughed. I loved talking with these other people, hearing their stories, and learning about their dreams. These people were my people – they were just like me.

And in the midst of the speakers and table conversations, something amazing happened. Being in the presence of like-minded people inspired a profound shift in me.

It's hard to explain how fast the shift occurred. I didn't expect it, but at that event, I fell head-over-heels in love with my dream.

Suddenly my dream wasn't some far-off, totally unrealistic, risky thing. It was right there in front of me. The minute I allowed myself to love the experience, I thought about those darn boxes. And something changed. In that moment, I decided to let go. I refused to hold on to my fears and doubts. If I was going anywhere with my training, I had to open up those boxes. I chose to quit being afraid of the questions running through my head.

You may be thinking, "That's it? After four months of drama, you just *decided* to open the boxes? Come on!"

Yes. That's pretty much the gist of it. Though I'd fought myself for months, I finally allowed myself to feel excited again. And that's when I realized that I was tired of being stuck. So, I chose to get un-stuck. It was one of the most powerful moments of my journey because I learned a very important lesson. "Stuck" is a feeling, not a circumstance. And the moment you confront that reality, the feeling loses its power over you.

> *You can focus on fear or hope,*
> *but you can't focus on both.*

The Courage Test requires you to choose. Where will you focus your energy? Decide now, because *you are* going to encounter "boxes" of your own. I don't know how your "boxes" will manifest themselves. But I do know that they will represent your biggest fears.

My question is: Will you open them? Will you have the courage to invest in yourself? Will you dig deep to create the exceptional life and future you want?

I know it's hard. I've been there. But take it from me. Nothing good can happen in your life if you allow yourself to stay stuck. Remember, stuck is a feeling, not a circumstance.

Stuck is a feeling, not a circumstance.

When you are confronted with fear and uncertainty, remember my box story. Love casts out fear. Focus on what you love. Your passion must become the driving force behind everything you do.

Happy Box Opening!

Control What You Can Control

Do you know how few people are actually living their dream? According to a 2012 study of 8,000 professionals on LinkedIn, less than one third of LinkedIn members are in their dream job or related field. That tells me that there are far too many people out there who are listening to that nasty little discouraging voice in their head.[5]

If you haven't encountered it already, you're going to hear the voice of doubt, too. It's going to ask you questions you can't answer and tell you all the reasons you can't follow your dreams. Be aware that this voice is coming. Choose to be prepared for it. When you find yourself worrying about what comes next, bring your mind back to *now*. You can't change the past or control the future. *The only thing you have power over is the present moment.* More people would chase their dreams if they came with a guarantee. But there are no guarantees.

You have to be willing to move forward anyway. When you're faced with doubts and fears, remind

---

[5] Basu, Sreeradha. "LinkedIn Research Reveals Data about the Top Childhood Dream Jobs." *The Economic Times*. November 19, 2012. http://articles.economictimes.indiatimes.com/2012-11-19/news/35203871_1_dream-job-childhood-dream-largest-professional-network.

yourself that you are in control of this moment. This moment, right in front of you. Remind yourself that you don't have to have all the steps planned out. You don't have to know all the answers. It's okay to be nervous, but it's *not* okay to let your nerves hold you hostage. If you want to live an exceptional life, you have to step up and take control!

"Fearlessness is like a muscle. I know from my own life that the more I exercise it, the more natural it becomes to not let my fears run me."

Arianna Huffington

Journal for the Journey

1. When has fear held you hostage in the past? What did it cost you?

_____

_____

_____

_____

2. When have you overcome fear in the past? What was the benefit?

_____

_____

_____

_____

3. What have you learned about pushing through fear in the past?

_____

_____

_____

_____

4. What limiting beliefs are holding you back right now?

_____

_____

_____

_____

5. How can you control the *present moment*? Why does this have power?

_____

_____

_____

_____

6. Do you believe that love casts out fear? Why or why not?

_____

_____

_____

_____

Affirmation

This is what I'm meant to do. I was designed to live a bigger life. I'm living a life of purpose and significance because I am willing to get out of my comfort zone. I love my life and the future I am building. I am willing to grow into it. I choose to confront my fears and take action to create the bigger life I was designed to live!

Signposts for the Journey

1. Stuck is a feeling, not a circumstance.

2. The moment you confront the reality that "stuck" is simply a feeling - the feeling loses its power.

3. You can focus on fear or hope, but you can't focus on both.

4. When you find yourself worrying about what comes next, bring your mind back to *the present moment.*

5. Love casts out fear. Let passion be your driving force.

"Dare to live the life you have dreamed for yourself. Go forward and make your dreams come true."

Ralph Waldo Emerson

Chapter 6:
Passing the Confidence Test

I had no idea what I was doing when I got there, but the coaching event changed my life. Up to that point, I'd been relying on myself to figure things out. Scared and feeling lost, I'd floundered because I had no idea how to build my business. But when I was at the coaching event, I learned that I couldn't rely solely on myself – I needed to reach out to others for guidance and mentorship. I also found the answers to my questions. Many of those answers came from the teachers leading the event. One of them was Paul Martinelli, now the president of The John Maxwell Team.

I'd never experienced a teacher like Paul. When I was around him, I not only felt inspired, but I began to believe that *I* could be successful in this business. Toward the end of the training, Paul described the mentorship program that he and his team were offering. He promised that their program would help me get the clarity I was so desperately seeking. But it wasn't cheap. It cost $6,000. Whew. Another $6,000? My heart sunk. I didn't have $6,000.

On the surface, it seemed like a bad decision. But my gut was telling me that I had to see this through. *This was my next step.*

Let me point out that I didn't know my next ten steps, or even the next five. All I knew was that this was my *next* step. See, this is the part of my journey that I used to gloss over. With reflection, I've learned the importance of this part of my experience. I was learning to trust myself.

By this point, I'd become a professional diver. In fact, I'd made a habit of diving first and asking questions later. Obviously, this wasn't the first time I'd followed my "gut." This entire dream-chasing process had been about following my instincts. But there's a difference between flying blind and flying scared. Up to this point, I'd been flying blind *and* scared. I was acting on faith, but was terrified of the outcome.

For the first time, I was acting on faith, yet I felt totally confident about my decision. Something shifted. I began to believe in myself and my ability to make my business a success. I no longer felt like I had to have all the perfect information, or the perfect network, or the perfect business plan. John C. Maxwell says, "If you wouldn't bet on you, then why should anyone else?" *This moment was about me learning to bet on myself.* There were variables that I couldn't control in my future, but the one thing I could control was me. I was in charge and I was going to *make* this work.

This may sound simple, but it was truly a breakthrough for me. The funny thing is that even though my circumstances hadn't changed, I was learning to believe in myself. And that's a powerful thing.

Sometimes the most important breakthroughs are internal rather than circumstantial.

The Confidence Test is all about learning to believe in and bet on yourself. I still didn't know *how* to make this business work, but through Paul's teachings and mentorship, I came to understand that I was resourced to find the answers I needed. For the first time, I owned my dream. This mental shift changed everything. My greatest hope is that you are coming to understand something important. *You are already resourced with everything you need to make your dream a reality.*

At one point, I had a friend ask me why I would wait to live the life of my dreams. He said, "Melissa, if this is truly your dream, then why wait?" You know what? He was right.

So, now it's my turn to ask you the same powerful question. What are you waiting for? There is no time like the present! Don't wait for validation. Don't wait for perfect timing. Don't wait to see the next

It's time for you to own your dream.

twelve steps in front of you. Just focus on your next step.

It's time for you to own your dream. Determine to see this journey through. Keep your eyes open and pay attention to your heart. Accept the fact that you don't need all the answers. Look for the next step. It's the only one you need.

Happy Confidence-Building!

Discovering Your Next Step

I don't know what you are struggling with right now. Perhaps it's a decision you've put off too long. Maybe it's how to best approach a situation that you've felt unsure about. Perhaps you've been avoiding the little voice inside you that's whispering, "This is *your* next step." I'm not sure what you're facing, but I know that you can't find clarity and direction when you are too busy to listen. Stop and get quiet so you can hear your intuition. Take a moment to ask yourself, "What does my intuition want me to know right now?"

Gary Klein, a psychologist who has devoted years to studying intuition, once said, "The longer we wait to defend our intuition, the less we will have to defend."

I think he's dead on. Your gut, or intuition, is there to guide you. If you find yourself arguing with your intuition, as I've done too many times, consciously choose to stop and listen. Investigate what your intuition is telling you, as well as why you are resisting it. This is a test, my friend. The people who live exceptional lives pass this test. It's your turn. Trust yourself! Your intuition will guide you.

"Men go abroad to wonder at the heights of mountains, at the huge waves of the sea, at the long courses of the rivers, at the vast compass of the ocean, at the circular motions of the stars, and they pass by themselves without wondering."

St. Augustine

Journal for the Journey

1. When has your "gut" feeling made a difference in your life?

_____

_____

_____

_____

2. Why is it important to follow your intuition?

_____

_____

_____

_____

3. When have you resisted your intuition in the past? What was the outcome?

_____

_____

_____

_____

4. What is your "gut" telling you right now? Don't answer quickly. Stop and dig into this question.

_____

_____

_____

_____

5. How could paying more attention to your intuition make a difference in your *pursuit*?

_____

_____

_____

_____

6. What is the next step for you? How could you take action on that "next step" this week?

_____

_____

_____

_____

Affirmation

I am resourced to take action on my dream. My intuition is leading me in the direction of my future. I choose to listen to my intuition, believing that it will guide me to my next step.

Signposts for the Journey

We rarely get clarity on anything beyond the next step of the journey, but the next step is enough.

1. You are already resourced with everything you need to make your dream a reality.

2. Sometimes the most important breakthroughs are internal rather than circumstantial.

3. Your gut, or intuition, is there to guide you to your next step.

4. The only way to get clarity is to get intentional about listening for the little voice inside you.

"Forget about the fast lane. If you really want to fly, harness your power to your passion. Honor your calling. Everybody has one. Trust your heart and success will come to you."

Oprah Winfrey

Stage 3:
Living Your Dream

Welcome to Stage 3!

Congratulations! You are entering the final stage of your journey: *Living Your Dream*. Stage 2 was all about overcoming the obstacles and internal roadblocks that may have held you back in the past. Those steps are a critical part of the process because they set you up for success in the final stage.

Stage 3 is about turning those steps into leaps and bounds. It's about taking the kind of massive action that creates measurable and sustainable results. It's about chasing your dreams with passion to create and live an exceptional life.

You crawled in Stage 1 and walked in Stage 2. Now it's time to run in Stage 3. This is where your journey becomes a *Hot Pursuit*. Here you learn to apply the principles and practices that build momentum. You align yourself with the resources and skills that take you to the next level. As you enter into your own *Hot Pursuit*, you begin to see the fruits of your commitment, courage, and confidence.

This is the stage where you begin living the dream that has settled down deep in your bones. It's time to buckle up, my friend, because this is where it gets really fun. Ready for the rubber to meet the road? Let's go!

Happy Travels!

Melissa V. West

Chapter 7:
Chasing Mentorship

When I got out my credit card and said "yes" to the $6,000 dollar mentorship program, I shouted a big, resounding "yes" to my dream. That "yes" gave me a sense of hope like I'd never felt before. For the first time, I didn't feel alone. My mentors were going to help me every step of the way. No wonder I felt more confident and in control!

That night, I slept like a baby. Wait, I take that back. Who made up that crazy statement? I have a baby so I know better than to say that! Anyway...let's just say, I felt peace. I didn't know how, but things were going to be okay.

The event ended and it was finally time to do what I should have done four months before. I flew home and dug into the boxes in my living room like a five-year-old on Christmas morning.

For the first time, those boxes were a *gift*. I took out all the material and laid it out on my floor. I wanted to look at every single thing. There were CDs and brochures, binders and scripts - all the building blocks I needed to start my business.

I felt so inspired by my new program and mentors that I quickly set a very ambitious goal. I didn't have a single paying client, but I was going to be a full-time coach in nine months. How was I going to do that? I had absolutely no clue, but thankfully, I had a team of mentors to help me. I turned to Paul. When I talked to him about my goal, a part of me expected him to laugh at me. Nine months! No one builds a business in nine months! Ha!

But he didn't laugh. Instead, he gave me some hard, but honest advice. He said, "Melissa, with such a tight timeline, you are going to have to make some major adjustments in the way you spend your time." He went on to tell me that I needed to devote every spare moment to my business. He gave me the unwelcome news that my social life was going to have to be put on hold. If I was serious about building my business, then I had to make decisions that reflected that commitment.

The first choice I made was to get up early. I'm not going to lie - it was *terrible*. I'm highly suspicious of people who wake up cheerful at 5:00 am. *Who does that?* It's still dark outside, and I'm a firm believer in waking up *after* the sun. But I wanted to succeed. So, I forced myself to set my alarm for 5:00 a.m. and worked on my business for two hours before I left for my day job. Then I added time during lunch breaks, after work, and on the weekends.

	Sunday	Monday	Tuesday	Wednesday	Thursday	Friday	Saturday
5:00 AM		Reading, Studying, Practicing	Reading, Studying, Practicing	Reading, Studying, Practicing	Reading, Studying, Practicing	Sleep in	
6:00 AM	Sleep in						Sleep in
7:00 AM							
8:00 AM							Mentorship Call
9:00 AM			Job		Job	Job	
10:00 AM							
11:00 AM	Family & Friends	Job		Job			
12:00 PM			Read		Read	Read	
1:00 PM							
2:00 PM			Job		Job	Job	
3:00 PM							Family & Friends
4:00 PM			Mentorship Call		Training Call		
5:00 PM	Content Dev., Marketing materials, Blogging, Emails, Studying	Personal Time	Personal Time	Personal Time	Personal Time		
6:00 PM							
7:00 PM						Family & Friends	
8:00 PM		Emails, Networking, Practicing	Emails, Networking, Practicing	Emails, Networking, Practicing	Emails, Networking, Practicing		
9:00 PM							

As part of my program, I had access to hours and hours of content and training material. I spent every spare minute reading, studying teaching material, practicing scripts, and writing emails. I put myself through each workshop as if I were a client. If you'd told me six months before that I would be working more than 20 hours per week on my business while still working my fulltime day job, I would have told you this was impossible. I didn't have that kind of time. But this is what I know: If you want something badly enough, you can find the time to make it happen. If you choose not to make scheduling decisions that align with your priorities, then you have to live with the results of that choice.

I've often heard it said that, "If you don't have time for something, it's not because you don't have time. It's because it isn't really a priority." I don't think that's true. Many of my clients and friends make decisions that fail to reflect their priorities, and it breaks my heart. Often, they feel that they have no choice. But we were created with a natural desire to live in harmony with our highest priorities. When we make decisions that don't align with those priorities, it causes stress and unhappiness. Ultimately, it can also cause a massive drain on our physical, relational, and emotional health.

Though I had to completely restructure my life, Paul was right. I needed to overhaul my life because I wasn't in alignment. Truthfully, I'd known that long before I knew what to do about it. Paul and his team helped me to create a life and business plan that reflected what mattered most to me. It wasn't easy, but it was an incredible time of growth. Looking back, I am so grateful for Paul's guidance. I know without a shadow of a doubt, I would not be where I am today without him.

My experience with Paul taught me firsthand the power of great mentors and coaches. In fact, I can say with total conviction that I will never be without coaches and mentors again. If you happen to be wondering about the difference between the two, let me give you a simple description from my perspective. Coaches help you develop self-awareness by asking careful and intentional questions. They listen closely so they can help you discover more *within* yourself. With coaching, you are the *source* of the information and answers. In a mentoring relationship, on the other hand, mentors are the source of information. They help you by teaching you from their own experience. They also share resources and information that help you on your journey. Both are invaluable.

When I decided to replace the income from my day job with a coaching career in nine months, my mentors helped me develop a plan. When I needed help developing the speaking, training, and coaching skills to build my business, my mentors taught me how to grow myself so that I was equipped to serve my clients. When I needed to get clarity around my vision, my mentors coached me to greater depths of personal discovery.

My decision to join the mentorship program was arguably the single most important decision I made in the pursuit of my dreams. Today, now being a faculty member and mentor for the John Maxwell Team is such a gift because I get to give back to those who are in the same place I was. I have the privilege of pouring into them the way Paul and my mentors did for me. These experiences have demonstrated an important truth.

> *One of the biggest mistakes people make as new entrepreneurs is to try to go it alone.*

Those who are in the closest proximity to you have the greatest influence over you.

One of the biggest mistakes people make as new entrepreneurs is to try to go it alone. Don't underestimate the value of learning from people who have already developed the skills that you need. If you want to break through to Stage 3: *Living Your*

Dream, then you need to surround yourself with the right people. Good mentors can help you avoid mistakes and maximize opportunities. They can have a tremendous impact on whether you fail or succeed.

This may be the most powerful advice I can give you: *Find mentors.* There will be a time when you will get discouraged. There will be a time when you take a wrong turn. There will be a time when you need to ask for help. This is why you need mentors. If you have to pay for mentorship, then pay for it. Quality mentors are worth every penny. An investment in yourself will pay dividends in the long run. Don't take this journey alone.

Happy Investing!

Finding a Mentor

Once they understand they need one, many people struggle with finding a mentor. They simply don't know *how*. In her article, "How to Find a Great Mentor," Forbes contributor, Kathy Caprino, says you should look for, "Inspiring people you're already interacting and working with now. They need to be people to whom you have already demonstrated your potential – who know how you think, act, communicate and contribute. And they have to like, trust and believe in you already. They also need to believe with absolute certainty that you'll put to great use all their input and feedback."

That's great advice. The question is – to whom have you demonstrated that you would be a good candidate for mentorship? Is there someone in your current network who might be willing to answer a few questions from time to time? If you don't have someone in your network, then consider paying for mentorship. There are many top level mentors who offer mentorship programs for a price. I highly recommend looking at all potential opportunities. There are mentors out there if you are willing to look for them!

When you are fortunate enough to find a mentor, treat the relationship with the respect it deserves. Come to each meeting prepared with good questions. Take copious notes. Put into practice what you learn. At each session, share with your mentor what you've applied from the last session. There is nothing more fulfilling to a mentor than the opportunity to see you grow from their mentorship. Be sure to demonstrate your willingness to take action on their advice. This can be a life-changing arrangement, so apply yourself completely to this opportunity!

"If you really want to do something, you'll find a way. If you don't, you'll find an excuse."

Jim Rohn

Journal for the Journey

1. Whom do you currently turn to for answers and encouragement?

_____

_____

_____

_____

2. If you don't have a mentor, who could you reach out to for guidance?

_____

_____

_____

_____

3. Do you believe that an investment in mentorship is "worth every penny?" Why or why not?

_____

_____

_____

_____

4. What are your five highest priorities? What matters most to you both personally and professionally?

_____

_____

_____

_____

5. Now, look at your calendar. Does your schedule reflect your highest priorities?

_____

_____

_____

_____

6. What evidence can you point to in order to demonstrate that you are fully committed to the pursuit of your dream?

_____

_____

_____

_____

7. What could you change that would allow you to make your dream a higher priority in your life and schedule?

_____

_____

_____

_____

Affirmation

I believe that I'm worthy of mentorship. I choose to invest in myself and my dream. I choose to align myself with people who will encourage me and help me reach my goals. I'm grateful for the resources that have already been put in place to help me, whether I've tapped into them yet or not. I move forward today with hope and confidence because the future belongs to me.

Signposts for the Journey

1. Good mentors can help you avoid mistakes and maximize opportunities.

2. More than anything else, what you need on this journey is hope.

3. Mentors can have an incredible impact on your success.

4. You will always make time for your highest priorities.

5. If you want to create momentum on your journey, you have to make choices that reflect your level of commitment.

"The only thing that can grow is the thing you give energy to."

Ralph Waldo Emerson

Chapter 8:
Chasing Opportunity

Sometimes I look back at my timeline and my decision to leave my day job in nine months, and I wonder, "What was I thinking?" That was a bold goal!

I didn't know it at the time, but that big, crazy decision was at the heart of my future success. Even though it was scary, it was the best thing that could have happened to me. From there, I had no choice but to get out of my comfort zone. If I was serious, I had to go for it!

Paul suggested that I start a mastermind group to begin teaching the program content. (If you aren't familiar with the concept of a mastermind group, it's simply a group of like-minded people who meet regularly to improve themselves and their lives. Often the members of the group have a specific goal, or emphasis, like leadership, personal growth, or entrepreneurship.) I was both excited and terrified by his suggestion. Yes, I would love to start teaching, but who in the world was going to come to my class? My entire social and professional circle knew me as a web administrator. On top of that, I had no authority in the personal growth space. I was just beginning to get my own life together, so why would other people trust me to teach and coach them?

But I was willing to try. Since I wasn't didn't want to stretch my neck out *too* far on my first attempt, I invited only family, friends, and colleagues – people who wouldn't be too hard on me if I messed the whole thing up. And since it was free, I knew they couldn't ask for their money back!

None of us knew what to expect, but even though it was a learning experience for me, it went better than I could have imagined. Week after week, those first seven people showed up with the intention and desire to grow. I was fortunate enough to be a part of their progress. It was confirmation. I was finally in the right place, doing the right thing, at the right time.

I *couldn't wait* to start my next group. Unfortunately, I'd exhausted my slim rolodex just to find my first seven participants. There was no one left to ask. Paul suggested I join a couple of professional networking groups to extend my circle. Plus, it would give me a chance to begin introducing myself as a coach, trainer, and speaker.

I felt like an awkward, bumbling mess at the first networking meeting. But with practice, it got easier. My new friends and acquaintances knew me *only* as a coach, trainer, and speaker. Even better, I began to get comfortable identifying myself as a coach. Thankfully, as my circle grew, it didn't take long to build enough interest to start a new mastermind group.

Then just when things were starting to move, a big, shiny door opened that I could never have anticipated. One morning, when I turned on 94WKTI in Milwaukee Wisconsin, two radio hosts were talking about goal-setting and how the right mindset is critical to goal achievement. As I listened, my first thought was, "I love this conversation!" My second was, "I could add value to this conversation!" Then came my gutsy third thought: "I should contact the radio station. They might let me be a guest on the show if I told them about my certification."

Boom, boom, boom. Those thoughts came right in a row, like lightning strikes. All positive. All encouraging. But then came the familiar nagging, negative voice behind them, saying, "Whoa, whoa, whoa. You don't even have a single paying client yet. What if they find out? What if you make a fool of yourself?"

Unfortunately, the negative voice didn't surprise me. That sad, sorry old voice had been hanging around all along. What did surprise me is that the negative voice had gotten quieter. Less aggressive. Less bossy. Less sure of itself.

Instead, the dominant voice in my head became my confident, positive, this-is-meant-to-be voice. That voiced asked, "What would Paul tell you to do?" Without a shadow of a doubt, I knew the answer. Paul would say, "Girl, this is your opportunity to shine. Go for it. Pick up the phone!"

I wish I could say I made the call, but I didn't. I sent an email instead. It's easier to get a rejection over email, right? Besides, I felt as if I could be brave since I assumed there was *no possible way* they would take me seriously. I mean, I was nobody. They were going to laugh when they saw my email, but I was okay with that. At least I would have tried!

I was totally, one hundred percent prepared for the rejection I knew was coming. That's why I almost choked on my Cheerios when I checked my email two days later. They replied. And not with the, "Thanks, but no thanks, shmuck," that I was expecting. I couldn't believe it, but they said yes. They asked me to come to the radio station so they could interview me for the show.

What?!? Really? That's it? You aren't going to test me or ask to see my certification or require me to do a fake session to prove I'm not an idiot? What if I *really am* a shmuck?!?

They were willing to give me a shot! I was ecstatic for all of five minutes, but then I almost had a heart attack. They were going to put me on the air, on a real radio station, with real people listening. It was going to be LIVE. As in, no do-overs. If I made a fool of myself, I was going to do it on LIVE radio. Clearly, I had not thought this through.

When the day came for me to do the segment, I was a complete wreck. Somehow, I dug deep and found the courage to put it all on the line. I planned to go in there, be myself, and do my best. If I failed, then I failed – but I absolutely refused to let my fear get the best of me. I was going to *fight* for my dream, and that meant I had to go for it, even if I was terrified.

Here's the good news. I did the show, and not only did I not make a fool of myself, but the show went really well. My co-hosts made it easy and the producer was so happy that he asked me to be the official coach for the morning show. Ha! Crazy, right? My teeny, tiny moment of courage turned into a great opportunity! From that point on, every couple of weeks I went to the station to talk about my favorite things: goal-setting, leadership, mindset, and psychology.

Soon after that, my phone started to ring. My business didn't explode overnight, but it did start to grow. Why? Because I quit waiting to *feel ready*. I quit hiding behind my notebooks and training materials. My dreams began to come true when I left my comfort zone and took a risk. Not once, not twice, but over and over. One courageous decision led to the next and doors began to open.

Here's what I've discovered after years of business as an entrepreneur. Doors don't open when you're timid, or when you play small, or when you talk yourself out of opportunities rather than into them.

There is no growth without risk, no progress without daring.

No matter what your dream is, your future depends on your willingness to get out of your comfort zone. That's why you have to *chase* your dreams with passion. Because there is no growth without risk, no progress without daring.

You must learn to jump in the path of opportunity.

If you are ready for things to happen in your life, then you must act. Take a risk. Make a decision. Your willingness to stretch yourself, to step outside your comfort zone, will determine your capacity to live an exceptional life.

What's on your heart or mind as you read these pages? Is there something you feel compelled to do, but haven't yet? Where in your life are you waiting to "feel" ready? What is *your* next "yes?"

I want to encourage you to take action. Don't be afraid to set bold goals. After all, shouldn't all our goals be bold? Shouldn't we be pushing ourselves to do more than we think we can? What's the point of setting goals we already know we can achieve?

Take some time to sit down and write out your goals. Be specific. What does your dream look like? I find it helpful to have an overarching vision—so think big and long-term—but I'm also a firm believer in setting incremental goals. What's your six month goal? What about your one month goal? What activities or action steps will help you move toward that goal? Prioritize those activities in your calendar. Then have the courage and commitment to pursue them with passion. Big dreams require bold goals! Opportunities won't come looking for you if you are unwilling to take action. You have to put yourself in a position for your own big, shiny door to open. Quit waiting. As Paul would tell you, it's *your* time to shine!

Ready, Set, Jump!

In his book, *The Five Secrets You Must Discover Before You Die,* author John Izzo interviews hundreds of people and shares what he learns from them about living well. He asked people ranging from 59 to105 years old what it meant to live a happy and meaningful life. One of the chapters that stayed with me is the one on living life with no regret.

One of the interviewees was Elsa, a woman who had grown up in Germany during World War II. As she looked back on her life, she said that the most important crossroads in her life were the times she had to act with courage even when she was afraid. Life was difficult in Germany after the war, so one of her biggest decisions was the choice to relocate to Canada at the age of twenty-two, even though she knew no one, had no job prospects, and didn't know the language. For her, it was a huge risk.

When Izzo asked her why she was able to take such a big chance, she said,

> "Whenever I had a risk I was considering, I would begin by imagining the highest possible good that could occur by taking that risk. I would imagine all the things that could be true if the risk worked out. Then I would imagine the worst possible thing that could happen if I took the risk. I would ask if I could handle the worst. Maybe I move to Canada and it does not work out. I wind up broke and alone. I knew I could always come back home. But then I imagined the highest possibility, that I would

start a new life, that I would make new friends, find love, and raise children in a new country. Then I held that image in front of me. Whenever I began wavering, I would imagine the greatest good I was striving for. I would always remind myself that walking away from the good that was possible was far worse than the consequences of failure."

What a great perspective to have on risk-taking! Another woman in the book told Izzo that when faced with a big decision, she would ask herself this question: "When I am an old woman sitting in my rocking chair thinking about my life, what decision will I wish I had made?"

When I keep that perspective in mind and hold the image of what I want in front of me, it becomes easier for me to step out in faith. I remind myself that opportunity will not come looking for me. My dreams won't come true if I choose to play it safe.

The same is true for you. Keep the image of what you want in front of you. Then, don't underestimate your ability to make it happen. Your future depends on your willingness to put your foot on the gas!

Friend, I don't know what you need to do next, but I know that you can't achieve your best life if you limit yourself. Self-doubt can paralyze you. Fear of failure can stop you in your tracks. Though your comfort zone is...well...comfortable, don't let yourself stay there. The best things in life happen just outside your comfort zone. Take a risk!

Happy Jumping!

"You cannot swim for new horizons until you have the courage to lose sight of the shore."

William Faulkner

Journal for the Journey

1. What is your six-month goal? What activities, or action steps, would get you closer to that goal? How can you prioritize those activities in your calendar?

_____

_____

_____

_____

2. What would you do differently if you were an older person, looking back on your life?

_____

_____

_____

_____

3. What is the best possible thing that could happen if you took the risk that is in front of you?

_____

_____

_____

_____

4. What might inaction cost if you choose not to take this risk?

_____

_____

_____

_____

5. Where in your life have you underestimated yourself and your ability? What was the cost of the risks you avoided?

_____

_____

_____

_____

6. Are you more likely to regret taking a risk or missing an opportunity in the future?

_____

_____

_____

_____

7. What would you do if you *knew* that you would succeed?

_____

_____

_____

_____

Affirmation

I refuse to limit what is possible in my own life. I will set bold goals and chase opportunity. I choose to create my future rather than wait for it.

Signposts for the Journey

1. You're missing out when you wait to "feel" ready. Quit waiting.

2. Sometimes all you need is one brief moment of courage.

3. There is no growth without risk, no progress without daring.

4. Big dreams require bold goals.

5. Make a habit of jumping in the path of opportunity.

"Whatever you can do, or dream you can, begin it. Boldness has genius, power, and magic in it."

Goethe

Chapter 9:
Chasing Momentum

Things were moving in the right direction, but I was far from making enough money to replace my day job. I'd begun to feel good in my role as a coach, but I was struggling when it came to sales and marketing. In fact, I just felt *icky* every time I tried to "sell" someone into a mastermind group. Why was this so hard? I firmly believed in what I was doing and that attending the classes were in my potential clients' best interests, but every single conversation was a struggle. I couldn't seem to get the right words to come, and I felt awkward and unsure of myself. This was no way to build a business!

It didn't take long to realize that if I was going to succeed, I needed to get comfortable talking to people about what I did. I needed to be able to invite someone to my mastermind group without a second thought. Timid and uncertain Melissa had to go!

One day, as I was sitting on my porch and reflecting about this challenge, I tried to figure out why I was feeling such uncertainty. Why was I struggling? I remember thinking back to my first real job in sales. When I was sixteen years old, I took a job going from door-to-door to sell newspaper subscriptions. I was given a sales script to memorize. Then a person on the newspaper staff drove me, along with several other kids, around a neighborhood to knock on doors and sell, sell, sell. I did this every day. At the time, I was working 12 hours per week, so that equated to 144 hours over the course of the summer. One hundred and forty-four hours of knocking on doors, smiling till my teeth hurt, and sweetly repeating that script over and over and over. I was a machine.

Guess how many subscriptions I sold over that *entire* summer? 100? 50? 25? Nope. ZERO. Nada. I worked all summer and didn't sell a single subscription. Now if that doesn't scare the sales right out of a kid, I'm not sure what does!

I learned to hate sales that summer. Obviously, it was not my gift! As I was reflecting on this experience, I began to put two and two together. I've carried this story – this belief that I'm not good at sales – around with me for a couple of decades. No wonder I was struggling! I was scared to death to experience the same feelings of rejection and failure. For all those years, this story had been shaping my view of myself and my abilities. It had crippled my ability to move forward. But this *problem* was totally unacceptable because I needed this business to work. Failure *was not* an option.

I kept asking myself, "How am I going to get around this? How am I going to solve this? What can I do to get rid of this feeling?" I didn't know, so I did what I always do when I don't know what else to do. I prayed, "Please God, work with me here. You know that I love this. This is it. This is me. This is my calling. If you could just send people to me, I'll take good care of them. I promise, I'll over-deliver. I'll go the second mile. I'll exceed their expectations. You just send them to me and I'll do the rest. Okay?"

I prayed and then I kept praying. God, send me the people. Send me the people. Send me the people.

Then, I wrote little affirmation cards and put them everywhere – on my bathroom mirror, on my refrigerator, and on the dashboard of my car.

Quality customers are seeking out my services. Those were the words that stared back at me all day long. I surrounded myself with little statements to help me build my belief. Over time, I did, in fact, begin to believe it. Quality clients were coming. I wasn't sure where or when or how they would find me, but I knew they *were* coming.

About this time, I remember talking to Paul about where I was in my business. I told him, "I have clients, Paul, but I need momentum. What do I do?" I remember like it was yesterday. Paul said, "Melissa, you understand coaching and you're good at it. What you don't understand is business. Quit focusing all your time and energy reading personal growth books. Now, you need to read about sales, marketing, finance, and leadership. To be successful in business, you must understand business. If you want to build momentum, then you need to build your business skills."

You build momentum when you build your skill set.

That was exactly the right advice. I poured myself into learning about growing my business. That same advice has served me well many times over the years. Every time I sense a weakness or limitation in my knowledge or abilities, I know it's time for me to find the resources to build my skill set.

At one point, once I'd finally created serious progress in my business, I had what felt like a catastrophic experience. I'd build my clientele and my business was exploding. That's the good news. The bad news is that I got comfortable with my success. I quit networking. I was no longer meeting new people and was fully depended on the clients I had. Somehow I had this illusion in my head that my clients would be my clients forever. Not knowing the average life cycle of my client, I learned the hard way that clients indeed do not stay forever. Over the course of a few months I went from a thriving business to a struggling business. I panicked. Things had been going so well. What was I going to do?

I gave myself an hour to fall apart, then I picked myself up, dusted myself off, and started trying to figure out what to do next. At the time, I had no choice but to go back to the drawing board and brush up on my fundamental business building skill-set. I read books about vision casting and problem-solving. I went to seminars on money and time management. I poured myself into learning from my mistake and getting back on track. I didn't ever want to be in that situation again.

That memory is still difficult for me to reflect on because in that moment, I felt like a fool. I didn't anticipate the worst case scenario and plan for it. But I should have. And I promised myself I would never make that mistake again.

As hard as my crash-and-burn experiences were, I'm grateful for them. My failures and mistakes made me a better coach, person, and entrepreneur. Each rough patch forced me to grow. My personal growth was the catalyst for the growth of my business.

I had my fair share of bumps and bruises along the way, but each one served my greater good. As I grew, my business grew. And nine months from the day I decided to leave my day job, I did just that. I DID IT! August 1, 2008 was my last day at my corporate IT job! I had accomplished the crazy goal I'd set for myself almost a year before. I can't even describe the joy I felt that day!

I remember walking to my car and taking one last look at the window of my office on the second floor. As "good" as the company was, I could never live an exceptional life in the cubicle where I'd spent so much of my time. That day was the day that changed my life. That day was the end of something good and the beginning of something wonderful. I felt it in every cell in my body.

I did a happy dance as I loaded my belongings in the back of my car.

But just as I was feeling pretty darn good about myself, that old, unfriendly voice came back, saying, "Guess what? You aren't getting a paycheck in two weeks. Are you sure you want to do this?"

That voice was a real buzz kill.

By this time, however, I knew how to silence it. I spoke right back to it and challenged it, saying, "I already know that this business works. I don't have to prove it anymore. I replaced my income and then some. This is the future I've worked so hard to build. Back off and let me live my dream!"

And sure enough, the voice backed off. I was elated. All the planning, the sacrifice, the baby steps, questions, the late nights and early mornings – were worth it. I had been preparing for *this* moment. *And it felt good!*

I woke up the next Monday as a woman on a mission. I had the whole day, yes, the whole day, from the minute I woke up to the minute I went to bed, to focus on the work I'd been called to do. For the first time, I was fully living my purpose and vision! It made my heart smile.

It's been almost 8 years since that day and I'm happy to say that my business is thriving. My practice is busier than it's ever been. In fact, I often have to turn away and refer business to others simply because I have no time to take on extra work. I'm truly blessed.

But you know what has held true? Whether my business was struggling or thriving, I had to keep growing. Do you remember the 2nd Truth? Your dream is always bigger than you. You have to keep growing. As you build your skill set, your potential expands. As your potential expands, so does the potential for your business.

> *As your dream grows, so should you.*

I'm not sure where you are on your journey or which skills and habits you need to build in order to live your dreams, but I do know that you can limit your dreams or expand them. Be intentional in the process of your growth. The payoff will be worth it!

Build Your Team to Help You Build Your Dream

Today, I still find myself returning to Paul's advice and it continues to make a difference in what I achieve. I am blessed to work with and for him on the John Maxwell Team. I constantly learn more and more from this brilliant man. My life has evolved in so many incredible and significant ways. I was also blessed to find and marry the man of my dreams three years ago. Last year we had a beautiful baby girl. Olivia is the light of my life. On top of that, we are excited to welcome a new member of the family in the coming months. Truly, my life has exceeded even my wildest dreams.

Now that my family is growing and I have more demands on my time, I've had to make some adjustments. Though I have a thriving coaching practice and am a faculty member with the John Maxwell Team, I'm first and foremost a mother and a wife. I love my business, but I know that my overall health and happiness depends on the quality of my family life. How can I tell people to live a life in alignment with their priorities if I don't follow my own advice?

If I've learned anything from my expanding business (and family) it is how difficult it can be to juggle it all. Thankfully, I've learned that I don't have to do it alone. So, my big "skill-building" focus this year has been on team-building.

Recently, I started reading books about how to stay in your "Sweet Spot," as my friend and fellow John Maxwell Team faculty member, Scott Fay, would say. In fact, his book, *Discover Your Sweet Spot*, helped me to identify my big overarching question: How do I limit myself to only the tasks and business activities that I enjoy the most, while delegating the rest?

As a result, I've intentionally focused on building my team around me. And let me be clear, I am not building a team of warm bodies; I am building a *dream team.* Every choice is intentional. I'm careful about who I bring on. I don't want people who are just looking for a paycheck; I seek out people who are passionate about what they do.

One of the best decisions I made was to bring on my good friend, writer, and thinking partner, Audrey Moralez. Knowing that my time and energy are limited, I've chosen to invest in her services. In fact, she's helping me put this book together. Contracting her services has made me more productive and profitable, but the big payoff is that it's made me happier and more fulfilled. And that is priceless at this stage in my life.

Sure, I could do all my own writing and content creation, but this is Audrey's area of expertise: her sweet spot. And every minute I spend on a project is a minute away from my husband, Chris, and Olivia. It's worth every penny because I get to stay in alignment with my highest priorities.

I've learned to rely on and appreciate my team because they give me margin. When my assistant is managing my blog and social media, my writer is helping with teaching/writing content, and my nanny is helping me at home, I gain breathing room. And I'm grateful for the value they all add to my life.

At first, it was difficult to give up control and delegate with confidence, but it's gotten easier with practice. When you find people who are really good at what they do, you may be amazed at how much time they can save you. When you realize that the product, the final output, is better than what you would have done yourself, it becomes clear: *Delegation is a beautiful thing.* In fact, I'm beginning to wonder if it's some sort of addiction. I feel like I might need to start a self-help group. We could call it ADA – Addicted to Delegation Anonymous.

If you haven't started, I recommend that you begin to think about who you need to bring on your team. Though your needs may be different than mine, I encourage you to develop a team-building mindset. Your impact will be limited as long as you go it alone. Focus your energy on taking yourself to the next level. Build your team, build your skill set, and build your dream!

"Unity is strength. When there is teamwork and collaboration, wonderful things can be achieved."

Mattie Stepanek

Journal for the Journey

1. Have you told yourself a "story" that limits your belief in your abilities? How does that story need to change?

_____

_____

_____

_____

2. Which skill, knowledge, or ability would take your business to the next level?

_____

_____

_____

_____

3. What could you do right now to improve yourself and strengthen your abilities as a leader, visionary, innovator, or entrepreneur?

_____

_____

_____

_____

4. Which tasks, projects, or services would you like to delegate to someone else, either now or in the future?

_____

_____

_____

_____

5. Who could you bring on your team that would allow you to stay in your "sweet spot?"

_____

_____

_____

_____

6. What would you gain if you were to delegate more often?

_____

_____

_____

_____

Affirmation

I take responsibility for my own growth. I commit to a lifetime of learning. I will be intentional with my time and schedule opportunities for learning into my calendar. My future depends on my ability to identify my greatest growth needs and then focus my energy on finding the resources to meet those needs. I am accountable for my learning and choose to make it a priority in my life.

Signposts for the Journey

Be aware of stories that you tell yourself and change the ones that don't serve you.

1. Determine where you need to grow in order to take your dream to the next level, then build your skill set with intention.

2. Delegation is a beautiful thing. Don't underestimate the value of a good team.

3. Your impact will be limited as long as you go it alone.

4. Build your team to help you build your dream.

"The more that you read, the more things you will know. The more you learn, the more places you'll go."
Dr. Seuss

Chapter 10:
It's Time to Start
Your Own Hot Pursuit

Before we come to the end of our journey together, I want to say thank you. Thank you for joining me and for letting me have a small part in your life as you pursue the life of your dreams.

I hope that this book has helped you and that you will refer to it over and over again as you continue your journey. Please read (and reread) these pages when you need a sense of inspiration or need to be challenged to take your next steps. I'll be the first to admit that this journey isn't easy. But it's worth it, my friend.

By now you've heard most of my story: the highs and lows, as well as the risks and rewards. It's been quite an experience. And it's far from over. As the horizon stretches before me, I'm no longer plagued by fear and self-doubt. Yes, I'm human and have my bad days, but they don't have the same hold on me anymore. I may not know what's around the next curve, but when I look to the future, I feel tremendous gratitude and excitement.

Recently, a friend of mine dropped by to check in with me. We hadn't seen each other in a while, and we were eager to catch up with one another. As I told her about all that was happening in my life and business, she commented on how far I had come. But the best moment of the entire conversation was the moment when she looked at me and said, "I'm amazed at all that's happened to you. But the thought that keeps coming to mind is that you're just a normal person. Don't take that the wrong way, but it seems like you should be different somehow. Better than me. Smarter than me. But you're just your normal, awesome self. It's obvious that you just kept putting one foot in front of another, and look where it's led you."

I laughed out loud. I loved her compliment because she was absolutely right. I'm not different. I don't have any special powers that you don't have. I didn't have an opportunity fairy sneak in and sprinkle magic dust on my head. I'm just a normal girl with a big dream who was willing to chase it. I faced the same obstacles as everyone else, but I chose to keep putting one foot in front of the other. In good times and bad, I kept moving forward.

Please, listen to me. I love your dream. I believe in your dream. I know you are meant to create and do wonderful things.

Don't let anything stop you. I named this book *Hot Pursuit* because your ability to make your dreams come true is dependent on your willingness to *chase* your dreams with passion. The future you envision isn't going to drop in your lap. It won't knock on your front door or run into you at the grocery store. You have to actively *pursue* it. Instead of settling for the good life, you must *race* toward the great life.

So, as we wrap up this final leg of the journey, I encourage you to keep your foot on the gas. It really is the secret to living the life of your dreams. As you move forward, I'd love to share some final tidbits that I believe will help you to keep racing toward your dream.

Enlist Support.

Looking back, I see all the times that it might have been tempting to quit. This hasn't been an easy road. One of my biggest challenges came in the form of a relationship that became strained when I began to pursue my dream. Let me warn you now – don't be surprised when some of your obstacles show up in the form of naysayers and doubters. In fact, those closest to you may be some of your harshest critics.

Early on, when I started spending all my time building my business, I found that my friends and family didn't understand my new passion. Honestly, I think they thought it would pass - just like skydiving and running marathons. I can't really blame them. It took me a while to find my way!

But one of my most painful moments was when I told someone very close to me about my dream and their response was…less than optimistic. They actually told me not to come back to them when my business failed because they were just going to tell me, "I told you so." Ouch. That stung.

Thankfully, even though it hurt, I understood where they were coming from. They were worried about me. They thought the risk was too big. I understood their fear, but it didn't make the lack of understanding any easier. I'm happy to say that though it was tough, we eventually worked through the situation. Now they are one of my biggest supporters.

If you experience something similar, try to understand the other person's point of view. They are worried about you. You are changing in front of their eyes and they have to adjust to the new you. Give them time. But by all means, do not give in to their limited thinking and beliefs!

This is why it's so important to surround yourself with positive people who support your dream. It's one of the best things you can do for yourself because you *are* going to encounter challenges along the way. Obstacles are inevitable. You are going to need people in your corner who can lift you up when you need it.

I don't know which obstacles you will face on your journey, but I do know this: Whatever they are and whenever they come, they can derail you. Surround yourself with encouragers who support you when times are tough.

Get Ready to Pivot.

For some reason, once I identified my dream, I expected it to stay the same. Now I realize how silly that is. Why wouldn't my dream evolve with me?

But I didn't see it coming. Just when I got my business going strong in Wisconsin, I realized that

I didn't want to stay there. I've always been close to my family and I missed my sister desperately. Her boys, my nephews, didn't even know me. One visit per year and a few phone calls each month weren't cutting it.

I made the very difficult decision to relocate to North Carolina from Wisconsin so that we could live close to one another. I'd worked hard to build my business, but I knew in my heart that once again, I wasn't living in alignment with my highest priorities. So, I started all over. The good news is that once I'd built my business in one place, I was able to learn from that experience and rebuild in North Carolina.

And here's the best news of all – if I hadn't made that decision, I wouldn't have met my incredible husband, Chris. I wouldn't be a mother to my beautiful, happy, sweet-spirited little girl or the new blessing on the way. So many wonderful things have come from my willingness to pivot when things changed for me.

I had a similar experience after I had my daughter Olivia. I'm very driven to be a present parent. I only get one shot at this motherhood thing and I don't want to miss any of the magic. Having her changed things. Suddenly, my business had to evolve to accommodate the new demands and opportunities of parenthood. I don't do any less, but I do choose to manage my time and energy differently. In this season of my life, I'm learning to pivot so that I can run my business in a way that allows me to be with my family as much as possible. I'm still passionate about my work, so I've decided to work smarter, not harder. For me, that means building a team to help me juggle all my responsibilities.

Sometimes I share this story with my clients because they seem to need *permission* to adjust their plan. Yes, by all means! Shift when you need to. This really *is* a journey that never ends. Unexpected circumstances will come up. You will have seasons where things need to change to accommodate other priorities. It's okay. Life happens – in both wonderful, and sometimes difficult, ways.

I don't know how you will need to adjust, but I'm absolutely certain that your priorities will change and that your dream will evolve over time. Just be ready to pivot when necessary.

Keep Saying Yes.

And last but not least – *keep* pursuing your dream! Never, ever quit chasing the exceptional life that you're meant to live. This is probably the most important piece of advice I can give you. Don't give up! Andy Andrews says that we must, "Persist without exception." I love that quote because there's so much wisdom in it. Here's what I know: some of your greatest sacrifices will become some of your greatest rewards.

If I didn't keep saying "yes," I wouldn't be coaching thousands of people around the world, traveling to transform countries with John C. Maxwell, and training people and organizations on how to live their best lives and build their best futures. If I hadn't continued to say "yes," I wouldn't have my amazing husband and beautiful baby girl. If I didn't say "yes," I wouldn't have the opportunity to be mentored by John C. Maxwell himself.

Every "yes" moved me closer to where I am now. Every "yes" I say now moves me closer to the future of my dreams.

"Yes" is the magic word that makes all the difference. Keep saying "yes," because the more you say yes, the greater your legacy will be. You may not have started this journey with a legacy in mind. In fact, I doubt you did. Most of us begin this journey because we want something for ourselves. We chase our dreams to create the future *we* want. But somewhere along the way that changes. There's a ripple effect when you chase your destiny, and the beautiful thing is that it creates a cascade of blessings that flows onto everyone around you. When you serve from your gifts, you bless your clients, friends, and teammates. You bless your family, because they get to see you fulfilled and living your dreams. You inspire people around you to believe that their dreams are possible.

The world needs you to pursue the best version of yourself and your future. I believe in you! It's time to embrace your journey, chase your dreams with passion, and live the exceptional life you have been designed to live. Let your legacy be one that makes a difference.

Never quit chasing your dreams!

Melissa V. West

10 Reasons to Start Your Hot Pursuit Today

1. You'll have experiences beyond your imagination.

2. You'll make new friends that share your passion.

3. You'll inspire others.

4. You'll serve from your gifts.

5. You'll feel fulfilled.

6. You'll learn and grow each day.

7. You'll feel hope for the future.

8. You'll make a difference.

9. You'll expand your capacity.

10. You'll look forward to waking up each day.

About the Author

Melissa V. West (Malueg) is the founder and CEO of Xtreme Results, LLC—a powerful catalyst for life transformation. She encourages business professionals to rediscover their passion and empowers them to create the amazing life of their dreams. She shares this message worldwide through coaching, training, mentoring, and keynote speaking.

In 2011, Melissa became business partners with John C. Maxwell—the #1 leadership guru in the world. Today she serves as a faculty member for his certification program. As part of this elite international team of 6, she has helped over 9,000 professionals from more than 130 countries build their own coaching, speaking, and training businesses.

Melissa holds a bachelor's degree in Management Information Systems from the University of Wisconsin-Milwaukee and is a graduate from the Institute for Professional Excellence in Coaching (IPEC) where she earned her Certified Professional Coach and Energy Leadership Index Master Practitioner accreditations.

Melissa lives with her husband Chris, daughter Olivia, and one on the way, in North Carolina. Connect with her at XtremeResultsCoaching.com

XtremeRESULTS | Think differently. Do differently.

Want More From Melissa?

Melissa is a powerful catalyst for business and life transformation. She encourages business professionals to rediscover their passion and empowers them to create the amazing life of their dreams. She shares this message worldwide through coaching,  training, mentoring, and keynote speaking.

AUTHOR – COACH – TRAINER – MENTOR – SPEAKER

If you would like to work more closely with Melissa, visit her at:
www.XtremeResultsCoaching.com

Daily Words of Wisdom

"Rather than depleting yourself with judgments about what you haven't done, who you could have become, why you haven't moved faster, or what you should have changed, redirect that energy toward the next big push – the one that takes you from good enough to better. The one that takes you from adequate to extraordinary. The one that helps you rise up from a low moment and helps you reach your personal best."

Oprah Winfrey

What amazing words! How can you look at this present moment, right now, as an opportunity to redirect your energy toward your next big success? You start from where you are – that's your starting point. Forget the coulda, woulda, shouldas... Start NOW. Be PRESENT and give today your personal best! Happy Personal Best!

Melissa V. West